Lee Andrew Hilyer, MLIS

Interlibrary Loan and Document Delivery: Best Practices for Operating and Managing Interlibrary Loan Services in All Libraries

Interlibrary Loan and Document Delivery: Best Practices for Operating and Managing Interlibrary Loan Services in All Libraries has been co-published simultaneously as *Journal of Interlibrary Loan, Document Delivery & Electronic Reserve*, Volume 16, Numbers 1/2 2006.

Pre-publication REVIEWS, COMMENTARIES, EVALUATIONS . . .

"Hilyer's book will serve as AN EXCELLENT PRIMER for those just beginning their ILL careers, and a refresher for those who have been at it for awhile. He PROVIDES CLEAR, CONCISE ANSWERS to most of the FAQs of ILL. The excellent and extensive resource section–taking up almost half the total length of the book–is one of the great assets of this first-rate work."

Randy Tibbits, MA, MLS
Document Delivery Team Leader
Rice University

The Haworth Information Press®
An Imprint of The Haworth Press, Inc.

Interlibrary Loan and Document Delivery: Best Practices for Operating and Managing Interlibrary Loan Services in All Libraries

Interlibrary Loan and Document Delivery: Best Practices for Operating and Managing Interlibrary Loan Services in All Libraries has been co-published simultaneously as *Journal of Interlibrary Loan, Document Delivery & Electronic Reserve*, Volume 16, Numbers 1/2 2006.

The _Journal of Interlibrary Loan, Document Delivery & Electronic Reserve™_ is the successor title to the _Journal of Interlibrary Loan, Document Delivery & Information Supply™,_** which changed title after Volume 14, Number 4, 2004. The _Journal of Interlibrary Loan, Document Delivery & Information Supply™_ was the successor title to the _Journal of Interlibrary Loan & Information Supply™,_* which changed title after Volume 3, Number 4, 1993. The _Journal of Interlibrary Loan, Document Delivery & Electronic Reserve™_, under its new title, begins with Volume 15, Number 1, 2004.

The Economics of Access versus Ownership: The Costs and Benefits of Access to Scholarly Articles via Interlibrary Loan and Journal Subscriptions, by Bruce R. Kingma, PhD (Vol. 6, No. 3, 1996). *"Presents a well-constructed and well-described study and a consequent set of conclusions about the cooperative economics of borrowing versus owning library journal subscriptions. . . A well-done and much needed book." (Catholic Library World)*

Information Brokers: Case Studies of Successful Ventures, by Alice Jane Holland Johnson, MLS (Vol. 5, No. 2, 1995). *"The insights in this compilation give practical overviews that are applicable to information professionals interested in becoming information brokers, starting their own brokerages, or adding this function to their existing library service." (Journal of Interlibrary Loan, Document Delivery & Information Supply)*

Interlibrary Loan of Alternative Format Materials: A Balanced Sourcebook, edited by Bruce S. Massis, MLS, MA and Winnie Vitzansky (Vol. 3, No. 1/2, 1993). *"Essential for interlibrary loan departments serving blind or visually handicapped patrons. . . . An enlightening survey of the state of the art in international lending of nonprint library materials." (Information Technology and Libraries)*

Interlibrary Loan and Document Delivery: Best Practices for Operating and Managing Interlibrary Loan Services in All Libraries

Lee Andrew Hilyer

Interlibrary Loan and Document Delivery: Best Practices for Operating and Managing Interlibrary Loan Services in All Libraries has been co-published simultaneously as *Journal of Interlibrary Loan, Document Delivery & Electronic Reserve*, Volume 16, Numbers 1/2 2006.

The Haworth Information Press®
An Imprint of The Haworth Press, Inc.

New York • London • Victoria (AU)
www.HaworthPress.com

Published by

The Haworth Information Press®, 10 Alice Street, Binghamton, NY 13904-1580 USA

The Haworth Information Press® is an imprint of The Haworth Press, Inc., 10 Alice Street, Binghamton, NY 13904-1580 USA.

Interlibrary Loan and Document Delivery: Best Practices for Operating and Managing Interlibrary Loan Services in All Libraries has been co-published simultaneously as *Journal of Interlibrary Loan, Document Delivery & Electronic Reserve*™, Volume 16, Numbers 1/2 2006.

The development, preparation, and publication of this work has been undertaken with great care. However, the publisher, employees, editors, and agents of The Haworth Press and all imprints of The Haworth Press, Inc., including The Haworth Medical Press® and Pharmaceutical Products Press®, are not responsible for any errors contained herein or for consequences that may ensue from use of materials or information contained in this work. With regard to case studies, identities and circumstances of individuals discussed herein have been changed to protect confidentiality. Any resemblance to actual persons, living or dead, is entirely coincidental.

The Haworth Press is committed to the dissemination of ideas and information according to the highest standards of intellectual freedom and the free exchange of ideas. Statements made and opinions expressed in this publication do not necessarily reflect the views of the Publisher, Directors, management, or staff of The Haworth Press, Inc., or an endorsement by them.

Cover design by Kerry E. Mack.

Library of Congress Cataloging-in-Publication Data

Hilyer, Lee Andrew.
Interlibrary loan and document delivery : best practices for operating and managing interlibrary loan services in all libraries / Lee Andrew Hilyer.
    p. cm.
    "Co-published simultaneously as Journal of interlibrary loan, document delivery & electronic reserve, volume 16, numbers 1/2 2006."
    Includes bibliographical references and index.
    ISBN-13: 978-0-7890-3128-0 (hc. : alk. paper)
    ISBN-10: 0-7890-3128-0 (hc. : alk. paper)
    ISBN-13: 978-0-7890-3129-7 (pbk. : alk. paper)
    ISBN-10: 0-7890-3129-9 (pbk. : alk. paper)
    1. Interlibrary loans. 2. Interlibrary loans–United States. 3. Document delivery. 4. Document delivery–United States. I. Journal of interlibrary loan, document delivery & electronic reserve. II. Title.

Z713 .H447 2006
025.6'2–dc22
                                 2005022257

Indexing, Abstracting & Website/Internet Coverage

This section provides you with a list of major indexing & abstracting services and other tools for bibliographic access. That is to say, each service began covering this periodical during the year noted in the right column. Most Websites which are listed below have indicated that they will either post, disseminate, compile, archive, cite or alert their own Website users with research-based content from this work. (This list is as current as the copyright date of this publication.)

Abstracting, Website/Indexing Coverage . . . . Year When Coverage Began

- *Academic Abstracts/CD-ROM*. 1995
- *Academic Search: database of 2,000 selected academic serials, updated monthly: EBSCO Publishing*. 1995
- *Academic Search Elite (EBSCO)*. 1995
- *Academic Search Premier (EBSCO)*
  <http://www.epnet.com/academic/acasearchprem.asp> 1995
- *Business Source Corporate: coverage of nearly 3,350 quality magazines and journals; designed to meet the diverse information needs of corporations; EBSCO Publishing*
  <http://www.epnet.com/corporate/bsourceçorp.asp>. 1995
- *Chartered Institute of Library and Information Professionals (CILIP) Group Newsletter, supplement to Health Libraries Review, official journal of LA HLG. Published quarterly by Blackwell Science*
  <http://www.blackwell-science.com/hlr/newsletter/>. 1998
- *Computer and Information Systems Abstracts <http://www.csa.com>* 2004
- *Current Cites [Digital Libraries] [Electronic Publishing] [Multimedia & Hypermedia] [Networks & Networking] [General]*
  <http://sunsite.berkeley.edu/CurrentCites/>. 2000
- *Elsevier Scopus <http://www.info.scopus.com>* 2005
- *FRANCIS. INIST/CNRS <http://www.inist.fr>* 1999
- *Google <http://www.google.com>* 2004
- *Google Scholar <http://scholar.google.com>* 2004

(continued)

(continued)

Special Bibliographic Notes related to special journal issues
(separates) and indexing/abstracting:

- indexing/abstracting services in this list will also cover material in any "separate" that is co-published simultaneously with Haworth's special thematic journal issue or DocuSerial. Indexing/abstracting usually covers material at the article/chapter level.
- monographic co-editions are intended for either non-subscribers or libraries which intend to purchase a second copy for their circulating collections.
- monographic co-editions are reported to all jobbers/wholesalers/approval plans. The source journal is listed as the "series" to assist the prevention of duplicate purchasing in the same manner utilized for books-in-series.
- to facilitate user/access services all indexing/abstracting services are encouraged to utilize the co-indexing entry note indicated at the bottom of the first page of each article/chapter/contribution.
- this is intended to assist a library user of any reference tool (whether print, electronic, online, or CD-ROM) to locate the monographic version if the library has purchased this version but not a subscription to the source journal.
- individual articles/chapters in any Haworth publication are also available through the Haworth Document Delivery Service (HDDS).

Interlibrary Loan and Document Delivery: Best Practices for Operating and Managing Interlibrary Loan Services in All Libraries

CONTENTS

APPENDICES

ABOUT THE AUTHOR

Lee Andrew Hilyer, MLIS, has spent his entire ten-year career in Interlibrary Loan in both corporate and academic settings. He has worked at corporate document delivery services, Rice University, the Houston Academy of Medicine–Texas Medical Center Library, and is now the Coordinator of Interlibrary Loan Services at the University of Houston.

He is a member of the American Library Association, ACRL, LITA, and serves on the Editorial Board of the *Journal of the Medical Library Association*. He also recently completed service on the OCLC Resource Sharing Advisory Committee.

He is currently pursuing a master's degree in education with a focus on instructional technology at the University of Houston. His current research interests include streamlining interlibrary loan operations, multimedia learning, and the evolution of the library profession.

Preface

Three years ago, I wrote a monograph entitled *Interlibrary Loan and Document Delivery in the Larger Academic Library*. This is not a new edition of that title. *Interlibrary Loan and Document Delivery: Best Practices for Operating and Managing Interlibrary Loan Services in All Libraries* is a different work entirely.

Interlibrary Loan and Document Delivery: Best Practices for Operating and Managing Interlibrary Loan Services in All Libraries has been extensively researched and rearranged to better reflect today's interlibrary loan department. All new material for all sizes of public and academic libraries has been added. New material has been added throughout this volume, covering ILLiad in more detail, discussing the issues of medical libraries, distance education, and other topics.

Part I is an introduction to interlibrary loan department operations and management, with the first chapter being a brief history of interlibrary loan.

Chapter 2 presents the "governing policies" for interlibrary loan from the National Code to local informal consortia arrangements.

Chapters 3 and 4 present expanded and updated information on borrowing and lending. The chapter on borrowing was extensively revised to include information on using ILLiad or another ILL management system, including new screenshots and descriptions of ILLiad workflows.

Chapter 5 presents a concise explanation of copyright law as it relates to Interlibrary Loan. A new discussion of electronic resource licensing is included.

Having just completed my fifth year as supervisor of a five-member interlibrary loan department, I have provided information in Chapter 6 on managing and evaluating an interlibrary loan department. Almost to-

[Haworth co-indexing entry note]: "Preface." Hilyer, Lee Andrew. Co-published simultaneously in *Journal of Interlibrary Loan, Document Delivery & Electronic Reserve* (The Haworth Information Press, an imprint of The Haworth Press, Inc.) Vol. 16, No. 1/2, 2006, pp. xxv-xxvi; and: *Interlibrary Loan and Document Delivery: Best Practices for Operating and Managing Interlibrary Loan Services in All Libraries* (Lee Andrew Hilyer) The Haworth Information Press, an imprint of The Haworth Press, Inc., 2006, pp. xvii-xviii. Single or multiple copies of this article are available for a fee from The Haworth Document Delivery Service [1-800-HAWORTH, 9:00 a.m. - 5:00 p.m. (EST). E-mail address: docdelivery@haworthpress.com].

tally new, Chapter 6 incorporates material statistics and costing. The section on management is entirely new.

Chapter 7 delves into some additional considerations for medical libraries and those libraries serving distance education students. A totally new chapter on additional considerations for the ILL department, distance education, and special issues in medical libraries was created.

Part II of this volume is an extensive listing of resources relevant to today's ILL, from excellent articles and books to websites, associations, and software packages. Arranged by subject, *Part II* is intended to serve as a handy desk reference when investigating new resources to assist you in solving problems and improving your interlibrary loan service.

Appendices A and B, concerning the National ILL Code, are repeated from the original text.

Appendix C (Statewide ILL Codes–Texas) is new.

Appendix D (Reciprocal Agreement) is slightly revised.

Appendix E (ILLiad E-Mail and Print Templates) is completely new.

Appendix F (ILL Technology Directory) is also completely new.

It has been my great pleasure to write this volume, and I sincerely hope that you find its information of use to you as you manage and improve one of the most exciting and challenging departments in any library.

Lee Andrew Hilyer

Acknowledgments

Special thanks go to Pam Cornell, for her insightful and helpful editing, and to the staff of the Houston Academy of Medicine-Texas Medical Center Library PC/ILL department, for their exceptional service and dedication to their patrons. Thanks also to my colleagues at Rice University, the University of Houston, the University of Texas-Medical Branch in Galveston, Texas A&M University, Houston Public Library, and the M. D. Anderson Cancer Center Research Medical Library.

[Haworth co-indexing entry note]: "Acknowledgments." Hilyer, Lee Andrew. Co-published simultaneously in *Journal of Interlibrary Loan, Document Delivery & Electronic Reserve* (The Haworth Information Press, an imprint of The Haworth Press, Inc.) Vol. 16, No. 1/2, 2006, p. xxvii; and: *Interlibrary Loan and Document Delivery: Best Practices for Operating and Managing Interlibrary Loan Services in All Libraries* (Lee Andrew Hilyer) The Haworth Information Press, an imprint of The Haworth Press, Inc., 2006, p. xix. Single or multiple copies of this article are available for a fee from The Haworth Document Delivery Service [1-800-HAWORTH, 9:00 a.m. - 5:00 p.m. (EST). E-mail address: docdelivery@haworthpress.com].

PART I:
INTERLIBRARY LOAN OPERATIONS

Chapter 1

Introduction to Interlibrary Loan

SUMMARY. Chapter 1 provides a brief background of ILL, discusses recent trends driving ILL activity, and recommends a programmed approach to understanding the ILL department through examination of goals/ mission statements, service expectations, patron preferences, and national, state, and local requirements. *[Article copies available for a fee from The Haworth Document Delivery Service: 1-800-HAWORTH. E-mail address: <docdelivery@haworthpress.com> Website: <http://www.HaworthPress.com> © 2006 by The Haworth Press, Inc. All rights reserved.]*

KEYWORDS. Background, definition of ILL, mission statements, organization, service policies

INTRODUCTION

Interlibrary Loan, or ILL, has a long history within libraries, with examples of interlibrary cooperation dating back hundreds of years (Smith

[Haworth co-indexing entry note]: "Introduction to Interlibrary Loan." Hilyer, Lee Andrew. Co-published simultaneously in *Journal of Interlibrary Loan, Document Delivery & Electronic Reserve* (The Haworth Information Press, an imprint of The Haworth Press, Inc.) Vol. 16, No. 1/2, 2006, pp. 1-10; and: *Interlibrary Loan and Document Delivery: Best Practices for Operating and Managing Interlibrary Loan Services in All Libraries* (Lee Andrew Hilyer) The Haworth Information Press, an imprint of The Haworth Press, Inc., 2006, pp. 1-10. Single or multiple copies of this article are available for a fee from The Haworth Document Delivery Service [1-800-HAWORTH, 9:00 a.m. - 5:00 p.m. (EST). E-mail address: docdelivery@haworthpress.com].

1993, 715). It has become the most common resource sharing activity within the library, though the scale of activity remained fairly small until the mid-1950s, when a standardized request form was introduced. The next decade saw increased development and availability of union catalogs and union lists of serial holdings and, in the 1970s, Interlibrary Loan was transformed again with the introduction of OCLC's ILL subsystem, which permitted libraries to electronically send and receive requests. Interlibrary Loan continues to evolve today with new developments, such as the implementation of international standards for transmitting and receiving requests (ISOILL 10160/10161), and electronic delivery of requested materials directly to patrons (ARIEL, Prospero, ILLiad, etc.).

"Traditionally, libraries and information centers depended on an ownership-of-materials model as the primary means of meeting customer information needs. ILL for books and photocopies of journal articles more or less filled any gaps between the local collections and local needs" (Evans 1995, 261). During the mid- to late-1990s, the perception of Interlibrary Loan as a "filler" measure began to change, as libraries accepted that their collections would not always be able to provide all of the materials necessary to meet their patrons' growing information needs.

Even into the first few years of the new millennium, trends identified over eleven years ago continue to drive the need for resource sharing activity and increasing demand for ILL services: ". . . (1) the growth of all forms of literature; (2) stemming from this, society's increasing reliance on information to enable it to function effectively; (3) inflation in the cost of materials coupled with increasing availability of technology, which have made it economically imperative to consider sharing resources" (Smith 1993, 715).

Emerging issues affecting ILL include the exponential growth of electronic access to journals and e-books, and the rise of "open access" materials, materials that, after publication, are openly accessible on the Web to anyone, anywhere, regardless of location or affiliation. BioMedCentral and the Public Library of Science are two examples of open access publishers seeking to migrate scholarly publishing to this new model.

ILL activity has already been affected by these two issues: overall DOCLINE® request traffic declined by 6% in fiscal year 2003, and Association of Research Libraries (ARL) statistics show mixed results: examining data from 1974-2003, ILL lending volume has been declining for the past few years, yet ILL borrowing continues to climb (see

<http://fisher.lib.virginia.edu/arl/index.html> for more information on ARL statistics).

INTERLIBRARY LOAN: A WORKING DEFINITION

Note: Interlibrary Loan (ILL) service in a library may operate under various names and acronyms: Interlibrary Borrowing, Interlibrary Lending, Interlibrary Services, Document Delivery, Resource Sharing, and others. Throughout this volume, I will use the terms "Interlibrary Loan" or "ILL" to refer to all of these services.

Interlibrary Loan is the sharing of materials among libraries, whether across town or across the globe. It is a service that provides access to the collections of libraries throughout the world. Interlibrary Loan service is primarily conducted library-to-library, on behalf of the patron (a mediated service). It is evolving and changing to incorporate more and more unmediated services, where the patron requests and receives material without any intervention by the ILL department. Interlibrary Loan provides access to materials not held in, or otherwise unavailable from, a library's collection.

Interlibrary Loan is comprised of two parts: borrowing and lending, and two parties: the borrowing or requesting library, and the lending or responding library. Most libraries function as both borrowers and lenders.

Included in this volume is a section (Chapter 7) discussing library photocopy services, sometimes commonly known as document delivery, which are usually handled by the ILL department. To avoid confusion, this book will refer to any service provided by a library to its patrons in which they *request copies of articles from the library's own collection* as a *Library Photocopy Service (LPS)*.

UNDERSTANDING
THE INTERLIBRARY LOAN DEPARTMENT

Mission Statements/Departmental Goals

Supervisors are encouraged to start the learning process by examining the library's mission statement, the departmental mission statement and/or a list of departmental goals. The library's mission statement is important in that it provides a rationale for the existence of the Interlibrary Loan Service. Additionally, the mission and goals of the parent organization (hospital, university, law firm, etc.) will have an impact on the service mission and goals of the ILL department.

> The mission of the Fondren Library of Rice University is to support the instructional, research, and public service programs of the University. . . . The collections and services of the Fondren Library . . . is more than a collection of books; it is an essential campus resource with knowledgeable staff and evolving information technologies where emerging and established scholars acquire information and gather in an atmosphere conducive to learning and other creative endeavors. (Fondren Library, Rice University)

The department's mission statement/statement of goals is also important, providing a more specific rationale:

> The mission of the Document Delivery Services department of Fondren Library is to support the instructional, research, and public services programs of Rice University by facilitating resource sharing for the ultimate benefit of all who seek knowledge. The department will recognize and respond to the information needs of its diverse client community, providing the highest levels of service . . . (DDS Department, Fondren Library)

> The HAM-TMC Interlibrary Loan service provides you with book/audiovisual loans and high-quality copies of documents (primarily journal articles and book chapters) from materials NOT OWNED by the HAM-TMC Library. (PC/ILL Department, HAM-TMC Library)

DEPARTMENTAL ORGANIZATION

Interlibrary Loan departments in academic or medical libraries usually handle both borrowing and lending tasks together, with some libraries splitting tasks between departments. *(Note: For purposes of clarity throughout the text, I will treat the ILL department as a separate entity within the library handling both borrowing and lending functions.)*

If the department is a separate entity, the ILL supervisor may encounter less administrative/managerial difficulties than if the operation is split among departments. No matter what the size or setup, however, the supervisor needs to know and understand the departmental organization.

ILL SERVICE FROM A PATRON PERSPECTIVE

Who is an ILL patron? In most libraries, an eligible patron is anyone with a library card in need of material that the library does not have, or which is currently unavailable. Faculty members and graduate students are generally the heaviest users of ILL services at academic libraries, with staff and undergraduates comprising a relatively small proportion of total volume.

Researchers and clinicians comprise the bulk of ILL requests at academic medical libraries, while a hospital library's ILL department may mainly serve physicians and nurses. Growth in the use of "evidence-based medicine" in academic health centers and hospitals may facilitate additional ILL use, since evidence-based medicine relies on the available clinical literature to help guide patient care and identify the most efficacious treatments.

Patrons are generally directed to Interlibrary Loan from other library departments, such as Reference and Circulation. Well-informed library colleagues can serve as an excellent bridge between ILL and the library's patrons. Departments should also promote themselves to their patrons, distributing flyers at relevant service points, advertising new services, and instructing heavy users on how to obtain the most value from Interlibrary Loan.

REVIEW YOUR REQUESTS

A simple review of incoming borrowing requests can yield a basic overview of the types of materials being requested by your patrons. Supervisors can analyze patrons' requesting habits to answer questions such as:

- How do my patrons use Interlibrary Loan?
- What departments are the heaviest users?
- Which patron category places the most requests (Faculty, Staff, Graduate, Undergraduate, Physician, Nurse, Other)?
- Are we meeting our patrons' expectations?

SERVICE EXPECTATIONS

In this age of Amazon.com and overnight delivery, patrons have much higher expectations of Interlibrary Loan than they did in the past.

Many departments have also "raised the bar" by implementing vast improvements to their workflows.

Service Levels

Patrons will want to know what service levels are available to them. If RUSH service is available, be sure it is clearly described. As is so often the case, there will be several patrons each semester that have left their research to the last minute and now expect the ILL department to procure 25 books for them in the next three days. Departments should clearly articulate their available service levels, so that patrons can plan accordingly.

Turnaround Time

In the past, many patrons considered Interlibrary Loan a "black hole"–requests were submitted and the requested material was never received. While ILL can still take longer than it should, vast improvements in the "ILL infrastructure" have made it possible for patrons to receive most materials within a week or less of request. Of course, incorrect or incomplete citations, improper procedures, and a lack of commitment to service can all increase turnaround time.

Most ILL librarians want to get materials to their patrons as quickly as possible and one to two weeks is the standard turnaround time communicated to patrons. In a study published in 1998, Mary Jackson found that the average turnaround time for ARL research and college libraries was 15.6 days (25). Initial data from Jackson's 2002 study indicates that turnaround time has decreased, dropping from 16.9 days to 9.29 days for loans, and from 14.9 days to 6.23 days for copies. Since the participants in the 2002 study differ from the 1996 group, additional analysis is being undertaken to compare data from the 46 libraries that participated in the 1996 and 2002 surveys (Jackson 2003, 22). However, the initial results indicate that, at least for ARL libraries, ILL service has seen significant improvements.

Supervisors should be realistic when communicating turnaround times to patrons, ideally basing turnaround times on a completed departmental service analysis.

EASE-OF-USE

Using Interlibrary Loan should be as easy as checking a book out from the library. Patrons should be able to quickly locate the request forms needed, ideally from a prominent link on your library's website. Instructions on the form should be simple and clear. Staff should be available to patrons by phone, e-mail, or in person in case of questions.

The pickup point for ILL materials should also be easily accessible–the Circulation desk, for example. If a patron has to overcome too many obstacles to request or receive ILL-obtained materials, they may end up forgoing the use of the material, to the detriment of their research. Or, they may bypass the library and its services altogether, instead preferring to order the book from Amazon.com or pick it up from the local bookstore.

COSTS

Patrons generally do not want to pay for Interlibrary Loan, or, if they are willing, the price they will pay is not enough to cover the costs. Jackson's 1998 study also queried patrons on the average price they would be willing to pay for an item requested through ILL. That cost was $2.71 (27). In a perfect world, ILL would be a completely subsidized service to library patrons, and it is at many institutions. However, that is not the reality in all academic libraries, and some departments must recoup the unsubsidized portion of the costs incurred to obtain an item through Interlibrary Loan. Medical libraries, especially, often must charge for ILL service in order to recover the associated costs.

If a library must charge, it should keep the fees as low as possible to allow the greatest number of patrons to benefit from the service. Whenever possible, overdue fines should not be charged, mainly because the added expense of tracking and collecting small fines often exceeds the amount collected.

PATRON BORROWING POLICY

A borrowing policy document that describes Interlibrary Loan services in detail should be available for patron review from the library's or the department's website. Paper copies should be available and can be distributed as part of library orientation. A patron borrowing policy should be as liberal as possible to allow patrons to derive maximum benefit from ILL.

The following is a sample policy:

INTERLIBRARY LOAN FREQUENTLY ASKED QUESTIONS (FAQ)
SMITHFIELD LIBRARY INTERLIBRARY LOAN DEPARTMENT

What Is Interlibrary Loan (ILL)?

Interlibrary Loan is a service through which patrons may request materials not owned by Smithfield Library.

Contact Information

Interlibrary Loan Department
Smithfield Library, Rm 321
Smith University
458 Johnson St.
Smith, TX 70011
713-555-1212
713-555-4134 (Fax)
ill@smithu.edu
http://www.smithu.edu/Library/ILL
Hours: 8 a.m.-5 p.m. M-F

Who Can Use ILL?

All Smith University faculty, staff and students may place ILL requests. Alumni and Smithfield Friends of the Library are not permitted to request materials through ILL. Patrons with "donor" cards may request up to 4 items per month via ILL.

What Types of Materials Are Available?

The ILL department will attempt to borrow whatever you request. Some items are more difficult to borrow and thus may take longer to arrive. These include current-year books, bound journal volumes, videotapes or CDs, foreign theses and dissertations, and microprint. If you would like further assistance before placing your request, please contact the ILL office.

Is There a Charge for ILL?

Requests for loans of material are made at no charge to the patron. There is a $2.00 charge per photocopy request made. Theses and dissertations not available for loan can be purchased for approximately $30.00.

How Do I Place a Request?

Log on to the ILLiad request management system and register to submit your ILL requests electronically! Go to http://illiad.smithfieldtx.edu and select the "Registration" link.
Paper request forms are also available at the Circulation Desk on the Mezzanine and at each of the Reference desks on levels 1, 2, 4 and 6. You can also e-mail your requests to us at reqill@smithu.edu. If you are using a FirstSearch database

(WorldCat, ArticleFirst or MLA), you can send your requests directly to us by clicking the "ILL" button.

Please be sure to provide us with as much information as possible to ensure the quickest processing and delivery of your materials. Please also provide us with your contact information and your preferred method-of-contact, as we want to be able to notify you as soon as your materials are ready.

How Long Does It Take?

Most loan requests are filled within one week; photocopies generally arrive in 2-3 days. Other materials may take longer, depending on the location of the supplying library and the method of delivery used. If you have a specific need date for your request, please stop by our office to discuss the request.

How Long Can I Keep the Material?

Photocopies, unless otherwise indicated, are yours to keep. Loans of books and other materials may generally be kept for three (3) weeks unless otherwise noted on the book strap. If you need to use the material longer, please use the ILLiad system to request a renewal.

Where Do I Pick Up My Materials?

Whenever possible, photocopies are delivered electronically through the ILLiad system. When you receive your e-mail notification, log in to ILLiad and select the "Retrieve My Articles" link to view and print your article.

You may pick up your materials in the ILL department during normal business hours (8 a.m.-5 p.m., M-F). If you are unable to pick your materials up during office hours, you may call and request that they be placed on the Circulation Hold shelf for pickup whenever the library is open.

Additional Information/Questions

For additional information on ILL, or if you have questions about your requests, feel free to contact us at the address above.

Thank You for Using Interlibrary Loan!

OTHER PROGRAMS/SERVICES

If the department administers any other programs for patrons, such as reciprocal borrowing privileges at other libraries, special consortial library cards, on-site borrowing, or reciprocal faculty borrowing programs, be sure that patrons have access to clear documentation or descriptions of each available service.

COPYRIGHT CONSIDERATIONS FOR PATRONS

Patrons must be made aware of their rights and responsibilities with respect to copyright law. Photocopy request forms (both paper and electronic) must prominently display the copyright warning. While copyright continues to be a major issue, there are still many patrons who are not fully aware of what they can request and/or how the material they have obtained through ILL can be used. The department should collaborate with other library departments to prepare documentation on ILL and copyright, or on copyright issues in general (for more information on copyright and ILL, see Chapter 5).

CONCLUSION

By now, you should have a basic overview of ILL and the patron borrowing policy, which serves as the cornerstone of effective and efficient ILL service. Chapter 2 continues your introduction to ILL by describing the many governing policies and regulations encountered daily in the ILL department.

RESOURCES

Consult the Background section in *Part II: Resources* for an annotated list of materials to help you learn more about ILL.

WORKS CITED

Evans, Edward G. 1995. *Developing Library and Information Center Collections.* Englewood, CO: Libraries Unlimited.

Document Delivery Services Department, Fondren Library, Rice University. 2001. Mission Statement [Originally written by Una Gourlay].

Fondren Library, Rice University. 2001. Fondren Library Mission Statement. <http://www.rice.edu/fondren/custsrvc/>.

Jackson, Mary E. 1998. Measuring the Performance of Interlibrary Loan Operations in North American Research and College Libraries. Washington, DC: Association of Research Libraries.

Jackson, Mary E. 2003. "Assessing ILL/DD Services Study: Initial Observations." ARL, no. 230/231: 21-22. <http://www.arl.org/newsltr/230/illdd.html).

PC/ILL Department, Houston Academy of Medicine–Texas Medical Center Library. 2004. About Interlibrary Loan. <http://resource.library.tmc.edu/ill/illfaq.php>.

Smith, Malcolm. 1993. Resource Sharing. In *World Encyclopedia of Library and Information Services,* ed. R. Wedgeworth. Chicago: American Library Association.

Chapter 2

Governing Policies for Interlibrary Loan

SUMMARY. ILL activity is governed by local, state, and national agreements and codes. Chapter 2 discusses the importance of national and statewide ILL codes of conduct, and also covers laws and regulations (confidentiality, the PATRIOT Act, HIPAA) germane to interlibrary loan. *[Article copies available for a fee from The Haworth Document Delivery Service: 1-800-HAWORTH. E-mail address: <docdelivery@haworthpress.com> Website: <http://www.HaworthPress.com> © 2006 by The Haworth Press, Inc. All rights reserved.]*

KEYWORDS. National Interlibrary Loan (ILL) Code, reciprocal agreements, confidentiality, records management, privacy, HIPAA (Health Insurance Portability and Accountability Act), USA PATRIOT Act, laws, regulations

Interlibrary Loan is covered by a number of national, international, and regional codes, which govern the general operation of ILL departments. Additionally, since 2002, a number of new laws and regulations which affect ILL services have come into force. It is the department supervisor's responsibility to understand and comply with the existing codes, laws, and regulations.

[Haworth co-indexing entry note]: "Governing Policies for Interlibrary Loan." Hilyer, Lee Andrew. Co-published simultaneously in *Journal of Interlibrary Loan, Document Delivery & Electronic Reserve* (The Haworth Information Press, an imprint of The Haworth Press, Inc.) Vol. 16, No. 1/2, 2006, pp. 11-15; and: *Interlibrary Loan and Document Delivery: Best Practices for Operating and Managing Interlibrary Loan Services in All Libraries* (Lee Andrew Hilyer) The Haworth Information Press, an imprint of The Haworth Press, Inc., 2006, pp. 11-15. Single or multiple copies of this article are available for a fee from The Haworth Document Delivery Service [1-800-HAWORTH, 9:00 a.m. - 5:00 p.m. (EST). E-mail address: docdelivery@haworthpress.com].

NATIONAL INTERLIBRARY LOAN CODE

The voluntary National Interlibrary Loan Code, revised in January 2001, governs ILL and provides a very broad policy for departmental operations. It is intended to foster open and liberal Interlibrary Loan policies. The committee in charge of revision did an excellent job on what was surely a difficult task, and the supplementary material they created explaining each proviso in the Code is extremely useful. (See Appendices A and B for more information.)

Departmental supervisors should be very familiar with the Code. Copies should be available to all staff members, and reviewed thoroughly with them. Paraprofessional borrowing and lending supervisors should be familiar with the Code and its implications for their daily work duties.

STATE AND LOCAL CODES

Libraries today must cope with tight budgets and increasing demand for services, which often necessitates the need for a group of libraries to band together to obtain favorable pricing or licensing terms for a particular resource or service. Combining in statewide or local networks helps to achieve cost savings and improves access to member libraries. ILL is often a strong component of resource sharing networks.

Many statewide library networks have written ILL policies, of which the department should be aware, that closely mirror the national code, with minor variations. In Texas, for example, most libraries belong to TexShare, a statewide multi-type library consortium. The ILL Working Group drafted a protocol that governs Interlibrary Loan activity among TexShare member libraries. One of the minor variations in the TexShare ILL protocol is the proviso that member libraries will not charge each other processing fees for lost or damaged materials.

Networks can also be formed on a more local level. HARLiC (The Houston Area Research Libraries' Consortium), for example, consists of eight Houston-area public, academic, and medical libraries. HARLiC members participate in a no-charge ILL program, a universal library card program, and formerly managed a local courier system (later subsumed by TExpress, Texas' statewide library courier system). (See Appendix C for examples of the state and local ILL codes.)

If the library is a member of a statewide or local network that has an ILL code in place, have copies available to staff and ensure that the department is familiar with them. There is the potential for loss of a valuable trading partner if provisions of an agreed-upon code are ignored.

CONSORTIA/LIBRARY NETWORKS

In addition to their state and local networks, many libraries are also members of consortia that are based on other factors, such as type of library, population served, or shared goals. For example, the library might be a member of the Greater Midwestern Library Alliance (GWLA, the South Central Academic Medical Libraries (SCAMeL) group, LVIS (Libraries Very Interested in Sharing), or any one of an infinite number of different library groupings.

Supervisors should be aware of the library's membership in any special library groups, especially those that include a resource sharing or ILL component, and should know what their department's rights and responsibilities are with respect to these codes.

Medical libraries also often come together as consortia. In the Southwest, for example, the South Central Academic Medical Libraries (SCAMeL) sets policies for ILL among its members, as well as facilitating group discounts to databases and services such as use of the Copyright Clearance Center. (See Chapter 7 for more information on the special organizational nature of medical library networks.)

RECIPROCAL AGREEMENTS

Even more specific than statewide or consortial agreements are reciprocal agreements. An ILL reciprocal agreement is an agreement between two libraries to provide each other with materials via ILL, usually at no cost to one another. Reciprocal agreements can also be used to specify service levels and often enable access to special services reserved only for reciprocal partner libraries. (See Appendix D for some sample reciprocal agreements.)

OTHER LAWS AND REGULATIONS

Confidentiality

"State law determines confidentiality of library patron records. Forty-eight states and the District of Columbia have confidentiality laws and the remaining two states (Hawaii and Kentucky) have opinions issued by their Attorneys General concerning privacy of library records" (Croft 2004, 17). Most of these laws refer to circulation and reference transactions, but in practice, most libraries consider ILL records as confidential and enact the necessary policies and procedures to ensure privacy.

ILL records should be treated like any other confidential documents and information contained within them should not be released without the patron's permission (except in the normal course of doing business, i.e., an OCLC request with a patron's name is transferred to library XYZ for fulfillment). This includes shredding paper records and taking steps to ensure that any electronic ILL request management systems (IMS) such as ILLiad or VDX are protected from hackers and kept secure. (See Chapter 5 for more information on paper and electronic records retention.)

Copyright

(See Chapter 5.) ·

Health Insurance Portability and Accountability Act of 1996 (HIPAA)

HIPAA became public law in 1996, but only recently have health care providers met many provisions of the Act. Its most relevant provisions for libraries deal with the privacy and confidentiality of medical records. Libraries who share facilities or even computer networks with health care facilities must comply. Medical libraries, in particular, must comply with HIPAA rules for ensuring the privacy and confidentiality of patient records.

ILL departments generally should see no basic changes in their day-to-day operations; however, there might be situations that arise in which HIPAA rules must be obeyed. Supervisors should consult with their administration or their institution's legal counsel for firm guidance on whether or not HIPAA rules apply.

USA PATRIOT Act

Enacted in 2002 in response to the terrorist attacks of September 11, 2001, the USA PATRIOT Act affects access to confidential library records and has been a controversial topic among librarians. The Act allows law enforcement officials to inquire about and/or seize library records (in some cases without subpoena or search warrant) without demonstration of probable cause. Librarians remain concerned about the Act since the lack of a requirement of probable cause leaves it open to misuse and to violations of individual rights, and because the Act imposes a gag order on any library staff involved, preventing them from discussing the incident.

Many libraries have adopted administrative policies and procedures for handling situations where a law enforcement official approaches library staff to request information or confidential library records. While ILL records have not generally been discussed, ILL department supervisors should nevertheless be aware of their parent library's policy on USA PATRIOT Act inquiries and instruct their staff accordingly.

RESOURCES

Consult the Laws and Regulations section in *Part II: Resources* for an annotated list of materials to help you learn more about the laws, codes, and regulations governing ILL service.

WORKS CITED

Croft, Janet Brennan. 2004. Confidentiality Basics. In *Legal Solutions in Electronic Reserves and the Electronic Delivery of Interlibrary Loan.* Binghamton, NY: The Haworth Press, Inc., 17-20.

Chapter 3

Borrowing

SUMMARY. Chapter 3 includes a detailed example of a typical work-day for staff handling interlibrary borrowing requests. Individual sections in Chapter 3 provide further detail on the borrowing workflow: receiving requests, searching for suppliers, handling problem requests, and cancellations. Processing requests throughout the entire borrowing lifecycle is discussed. *[Article copies available for a fee from The Haworth Document Delivery Service: 1-800-HAWORTH. E-mail address: <docdelivery@haworthpress.com> Website: <http://www.HaworthPress.com> © 2006 by The Haworth Press, Inc. All rights reserved.]*

KEYWORDS. ILL borrowing, daily routine, verification, OCLC ILLiad, ILL management systems, procedures, request forms

Now that you have had a brief introduction to the policies and regulations governing ILL, let's move on to borrowing and take a brief look at the ILL landscape in the early 21st century.

SAMPLE DAILY TIMELINE

What follows is an example of a typical workday for staff handling interlibrary borrowing duties. While the situation will vary, this sched-

---

[Haworth co-indexing entry note]: "Borrowing." Hilyer, Lee Andrew. Co-published simultaneously in *Journal of Interlibrary Loan, Document Delivery & Electronic Reserve* (The Haworth Information Press, an imprint of The Haworth Press, Inc.) Vol. 16, No. 1/2, 2006, pp. 17-39; and: *Interlibrary Loan and Document Delivery: Best Practices for Operating and Managing Interlibrary Loan Services in All Libraries* (Lee Andrew Hilyer) The Haworth Information Press, an imprint of The Haworth Press, Inc., 2006, pp. 17-39. Single or multiple copies of this article are available for a fee from The Haworth Document Delivery Service [1-800-HAWORTH, 9:00 a.m. - 5:00 p.m. (EST). E-mail address: docdelivery@haworthpress.com].

ule and description will help provide basic insight on the day-to-day tasks associated with ILL borrowing. A wide range of staff may perform these duties, from full-time professional staff to part-time student assistants.

Morning Routines

Mornings are usually spent reviewing the day's requests and checking on any overnight processes performed.

6:00 a.m.   ILLiad Connector completes a scheduled download of the latest updates to any active borrowing requests on the OCLC ILL subsystem.
7:30 a.m.   Borrowing staff arrive and log in to their workstations.
7:45 a.m.   Staff check departmental e-mail mailbox; sort and distribute messages.

New Requests

Incoming patron requests need to be reviewed. How the department accesses these requests will depend on the procedures and technologies employed in the department. For some, this will merely involve checking a queue list in an ILL management system (IMS) such as ILLiad or Clio, electronically reviewing each new request without generating any unneeded paper forms. For others, this process will involve the downloading and printing of e-mailed or web-created forms.

Staff may spend some time reviewing these requests for patron eligibility, legibility, and completeness of bibliographic information, noting any special instructions or any deadlines the patron has set for receipt of the material.

8:00 a.m.   Log in to ILLiad to review request queues.
8:05 a.m.   Grab a nice cup of coffee.
8:15 a.m.   Review new ILLiad registrations for eligibility, completeness, etc. (Upon completion, ILLiad automatically notifies new users by e-mail that their registrations have been accepted.)

Searching New Requests

After reviewing the day's workload of new requests, borrowing staff members plan their day accordingly. If there is a backlog of orders from the previous day, they will attend to those items first, along with any RUSH or other special service orders.

8:30 a.m.   Review and Process incoming borrowing requests.
Today's queue includes:
12 awaiting copyright compliance
7 regular service requests
5 RUSH service requests
1 Super Rush service request (Super Rush and RUSH service requests are handled first.)

Requests in the ILLiad *Awaiting Copyright Compliance* queue must first be checked against the ILLiad copyright database for compliance. ILL management systems (IMS) like ILLiad and Clio keep count of the number of times a particular journal is requested. When that number exceeds the suggested five copies, users can then pay the copyright immediately through a web link with the Copyright Clearance Center.

Borrowing staff process each request using the OCLC Live Link within ILLiad or through the National Library of Medicine's DOCLINE® service. Requests for material owned by the Library are reviewed, and then either requested through DOCLINE or OCLC, or are transferred to the Document Delivery module in ILLiad.

Locating Bibliographic Records and Potential Suppliers

After reviewing new requests, the borrowing procedure continues with the search for matching bibliographic records and the location of potential suppliers. Staff will generally check any available bibliographic utilities first, such as OCLC or DOCLINE.

A bibliographic utility usually consists of a union catalog of bibliographic records with additional services or systems offered to add additional "value" to those records. The ILL department uses OCLC ILL and/or DOCLINE to send and receive Interlibrary Loan requests based on those bibliographic records.

If a record matching the patron's request is found, then staff will usually create, edit, and submit requests to other suppliers via that utility's ILL service. Occasionally they may use the utility solely for verification purposes, with the actual request to be sent via a different method.

If a request cannot be submitted through a bibliographic utility, staff will often check the online catalogs (OPACs) of other libraries or search databases or indexes to verify correctness of provided information and to locate potential suppliers for requested materials.

Verification

If standard verification/location resources are exhausted, staff can occasionally "blind route" something to a supplier who may have the material needed. For example, some libraries do not catalog their theses and dissertations and thus bibliographic records for them are not readily available. The librarian can route the request to the library of the university granting the degree, on the off-chance that the dissertation or thesis may be available for loan.

Staff can also "set aside" requests for further research/verification. In ILLiad, for example, departments can set up a custom queue to catch any requests requiring extensive treatment. The HAM-TMC Library ILL department, for example, uses an "Awaiting Extensive Searching" queue to "park" any difficult or incorrect citations.

The ILL librarian then usually reviews the queue and attempts to verify the citation or identify potential lenders for the material.

Throughout the day, borrowing staff members respond to patrons in a variety of ways: by telephone, by e-mail, or in person. If the ILL department has a service desk, borrowing staff members may rotate hours at the service desk, assisting patrons with their materials and fielding service queries, including "status checks." Patrons will often call in to check on the whereabouts and expected delivery time of their requests. With an IMS that contains accurate data, staff can provide patrons with status checks quickly and efficiently. Even better, some departments don't use staff time to provide status checks—their IMS does it for them, with password-protected web pages that allow patrons to check on the status of their own orders—in real time!

Additionally, staff will handle unfilled and conditional requests on either DOCLINE or OCLC, performing additional verification or processing if necessary.

If the request is *conditional*, staff will review the conditions and respond accordingly. For example, the cost to deliver a document may exceed the library's stated maximum cost. The lending library is extending the courtesy of checking with the borrowing library to see if they indeed want to pay the higher cost, or look elsewhere for the material.

If the request is *unfilled*, staff have a few options: they can resubmit the request if there are additional potential lenders, or they may transfer the request to another system (i.e., OCLC → DOCLINE and vice-versa) for potential fulfillment. Yet another option is cancellation, though ILL librarians pride themselves on being able to find the most elusive materials.

Both OCLC ILL and DOCLINE permit lenders to indicate a "reason-for-no," such as "Not on Shelf," or "At Bindery." Users can access this transaction history to review the transaction and re-route the request to a new lender.

10:30 a.m.   Morning mail arrives; received materials are unpacked and prepared for processing.

Incoming Materials Processing

Processing of materials is another task to be performed during the borrowing workday. Depending upon available delivery services, the department may receive shipments of UPS, FedEx, and U.S. Mail materials at one time, or the department may receive individual deliveries throughout the workday. Material is usually unpacked and any paperwork or documentation is kept with the material.

Many libraries choose to reuse shipping materials. While it is not recommended, it is nonetheless a common procedure in most academic libraries. If the department chooses to reuse packaging materials, it is recommended that only envelopes and other packaging in the best condition be kept.

Receiving/Processing Materials

Staff or students will match up received materials with requests. They may do this by pulling paper forms from a file or by simply keying in the ILL transaction number into an IMS (Clio, ILLiad, ILL Manager) and selecting the "Received" update option after verifying that the correct material has been supplied.

For photocopies, staff might check their ARIEL receiving station to see what requested articles have been delivered overnight to the department. Records for these requests will then be updated to a "Received" status, either directly on a bibliographic utility (OCLC, RLIN), or in the department's IMS. Records updated in an IMS are often batch-transferred to the bibliographic utility on a scheduled basis, usually at the end of the workday.

Depending on installed technology and procedures, a staff member might transfer these received articles directly to a secure website for patron pickup, rather than printing them off for physical delivery to the patron.

For books, staff may place a strap around the received book, usually noting the patron's last name, the ILL transaction number, the OCLC or RLIN symbol of the supplying library, and a due date (these data elements vary with local practice). The original request form may be placed in the book for the patron to sign when they pick up. The ILL librarian or the member of the department who handles accounting matters generally puts any accompanying invoices or statements aside for review.

Throughout the night and early morning, the ARIEL station has been sending and receiving material to and from libraries across the country.

11:00 a.m.   At a separate workstation with ILLiad and ARIEL, borrowing staff review and process materials bound for electronic delivery.

Staff performs a "quality check" of each received document, checking for quality and completeness. Upon "acceptance" of the received document, ILLiad converts the document from TIFF to PDF format, copies the file to a web server, then sends an e-mail notification to the patron that the material is ready for pickup.

1:00 p.m.   ILLiad Connector completes a scheduled download of the latest updates to any active borrowing requests on the OCLC ILL subsystem. *(Connector updates ensure patrons have up-to-date status information on the whereabouts of their requests.)*

1:30 p.m.   Lunchtime!

2:00 p.m.   Above cycle repeats (with daily variation) in the afternoon.

Delivery/Pickup of Materials

After processing is complete, staff will notify patrons that they have materials ready for pickup. Notification is usually done by e-mail, though some departments notify by mail or by phone. When notification is sent, materials may be placed on a "hold" shelf in alphabetical order by patron's last name to await pickup. The department may also deliver materials via campus or U.S. mail, so stuffing envelopes and addressing packages might likely be an additional daily duty.

4:30 p.m. Before leaving for the day, borrowing staff activate the automatic e-mail notification in ILLiad to ensure that all patrons receive notice that their materials have arrived and are ready for use.

6:00 p.m. ILLiad Connector program completes its scheduled download of the latest information on active borrowing requests on the OCLC ILL subsystem. Additionally, any updates to existing requests (Returned, Received, etc.) are transferred back to OCLC so that the two systems remain synchronized.

BORROWING PROCEDURES AND WORKFLOW

Interlibrary borrowing departments handle large amounts of material, so efficient workflows and streamlined procedures are essential. This section provides some basic examples, guidelines, and suggestions for borrowing operations.

Request Forms

The first step in the Interlibrary Loan process is the generation or creation of an ILL request. The library's patrons may create requests or ILL staff may create requests on behalf of those patrons. Requests generally are submitted by the following methods:

- Electronic forms
- Links from databases or other electronic resources (e.g., FirstSearch)
- Paper Forms
  - ALA-approved ILL forms can be downloaded from ALA's website:
    - PDF (http://www.ala.org/ala/rusa/rusaprotools/referenceguide/illformprint.pdf)

- WORD DOC
  (http://www.ala.org/ala/rusa/rusaprotools/referenceguide/
  illformprint.doc)

Electronic Forms

As identified in Mary Jackson's ARL ILL study (1998), high-performing operations were notable for their use of electronic requesting systems. Additionally, the burden of keying in requests for ILL service is shifted to the patron, which frees up valuable staff time for processing and handling more difficult requests.

There are numerous IMS software products available (see Technology section later in this chapter) that include a request module as part of the package. Most of these modules are web-based and submit data to a back-end database system. Many products also have the ability to print out formatted ALA forms.

Figures 1-5 are some examples of ILLiad web forms for ILL services.

FIGURE 1. Customized ILLiad Logon Screen for the HAM-TMC Library

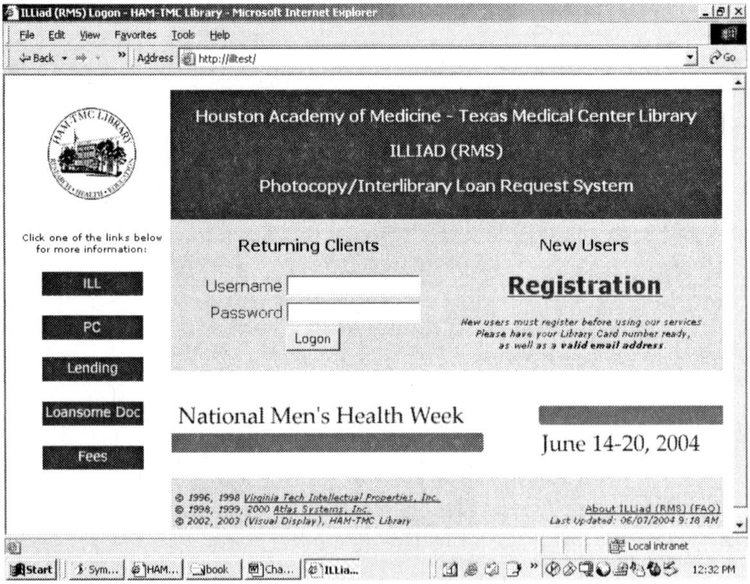

Screen reprinted with permission.

FIGURE 2. ILLiad Main Menu–HAM-TMC Library

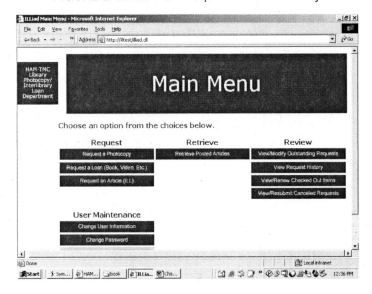

FIGURE 3. ILLiad Article Request Form–HAM-TMC Library (Top)

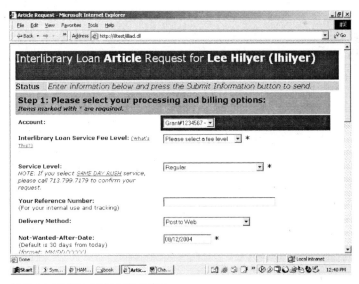

Screens reprinted with permission.

FIGURE 4. ILLiad Article Request Form–HAM-TMC Library (Middle)

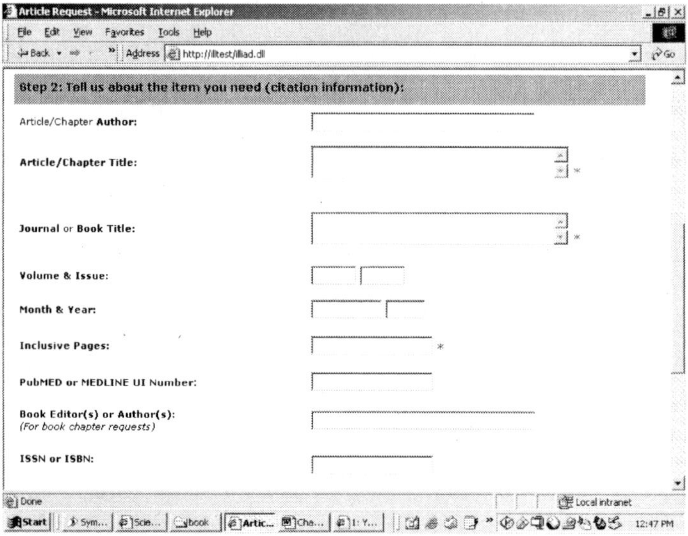

FIGURE 5. ILLiad Article Request Form–HAM-TMC Library (Bottom)

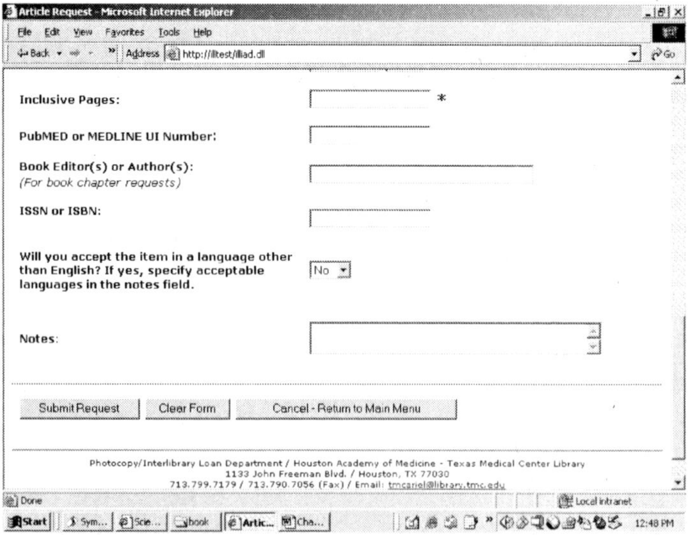

Screens reprinted with permission.

Links from Other Services

In addition to paper and electronic forms, some vendors provide additional services that enable patrons to request materials via ILL without having to leave the particular database or resource they are searching in. OCLC's FirstSearch service, for example, provides the ILL Direct link, which enables patrons to request materials identified while searching a FirstSearch database such as WorldCat, CINAHL, ERIC, or Agricola.

Searching for Suppliers

After initial printing or preparation of new requests, some departments will conduct an initial "review" of borrowing requests, though most departments "review" pending requests as they are searching for suppliers for the material.

As mentioned earlier, most ILL operations utilize one or more of the bibliographic utilities like OCLC, DOCLINE, or RLIN. Bibliographic utilities offer powerful systems for locating materials and resources and for requesting those materials from other libraries. If the initial bibliographic utility search is not successful, staff will often check a number of additional resources such as those described later in this chapter.

Verification

There will be times when bibliographic records or potential suppliers for patron requests are not easily located. These more difficult requests are usually passed to the ILL librarian or to a reference librarian for further research. The first step in verification is to review the bibliographic citation for completeness and accuracy.

Everyone has a different perception of what a "complete" citation is. A possible working definition of a "complete citation" is: a citation that allows ILL staff to locate and obtain the material that the patron needs. This will vary greatly, depending on the type of material requested.

Example: Biochem. Biophys. Acta. 13, 754-78. Johnson.

The journal title (abbreviated), the volume (?), a page range, and an author are provided. The issue number, the date, and an article title are missing. Reference lists, however, especially those found in scientific articles, often do not provide extensive citation information.

If, after reviewing the citation, the staff member feels there is not enough information to submit the request to a potential supplier, one option is to contact the patron to discuss the request and/or to request additional information. If there is adequate information, then submit the request to a potential supplier if one can be located, though the department may have to more fully verify the request should it return unfilled.

Verification is a challenging and potentially frustrating activity for ILL staff. ILL librarians love being able to find materials for patrons and surprising them with the items that they never thought they would be able to obtain. On the other hand, it can also be a lesson in frustration, as murky citations refuse to give up their secrets, even after repeated attempts.

Web-based request forms eliminate much of the guesswork related to patrons' handwriting, while other difficulties can be remedied by clear instructions on your request forms and by encouraging the use of services like OCLC's FirstSearch that transfer full bibliographic information from database records into ILL requests.

Verification is both a skill and an art. ILL staff should be encouraged to utilize a wide range of tools and strategies for verification and to share their expertise with other staff members.

Citation Difficulties

Abbreviations

Abbreviations can often be difficult and a source of confusion when requesting materials. Database creators often provide abbreviation and full title lists for the serials indexed in their databases (Medline/PubMed, for example), and there are numerous print sources available for deciphering abbreviations.

Lack of Specific Date Information

If the date is omitted, it may be difficult to locate requested material, especially if there are multiple editions of an item.

Database Citation Displays

With so many different citation formats used by various database vendors, patrons can sometimes confuse parts of the citation, or omit important pieces of the citation altogether.

Re-Verifying Database Citations

Most patrons are searching the library's own databases. Many times the likely database the patron used can be determined simply by reviewing the subject matter of the request. For example, if the request deals with languages or literature, try the Modern Language Association (MLA) database. Likewise, if the request is for a government document, try the GPO Monthly Catalog or the MARCIVE Web Docs database. Medical librarians typically receive citations from the MEDLINE database.

Catalogs

If the patron has requested an item for which there are no records on OCLC or RLIN, staff members may try searching some of the larger library system catalogs, such as MELVYL (California libraries), the British Library Public Catalogue, the Library of Congress catalog, and others.

Print Resources

Especially useful for older citations, the paper editions of *Chemical Abstracts*, INSPEC (*Physics Abstracts*), *MLA*, and many others can prove to be rich verification sources.

Search Engines

Internet search engines have become invaluable resources for many ILL departments. Google can be a rich source of information for verifications, as can many of the other available search engines.

Search engines seem to be more useful in confirming or adding to citation details than in locating actual suppliers. However, the requested item itself can sometimes be located online in PDF, HTML, or some other format. The ILL department should decide whether it will print out these materials and deliver them to patrons, or if it will simply cancel the request and inform the patron of the URL of the requested material.

CANCELLATIONS

Libraries should cancel requests only if the patron requests the cancellation or if all avenues for potential supply of the item have been exhausted. Many departments notify patrons of canceled requests using a standard form such as the one shown in Figure 6.

ILLiad and other IMS systems can be configured to automatically e-mail the patron when a request has been canceled (see Appendix E for a sample of an ILLiad e-mail cancellation notice).

MANAGING REQUEST FILES

Requests for ILL service are "updated" as they move through the ILL process from creation to completion. Likewise, the actual paper forms or electronic records are updated and tracked throughout this cycle. Many ILL departments have made great strides toward the "paperless" office while others remain committed to their paper files. How "paperless" the ILL department becomes is largely a matter of technology coupled with the comfort level of the department and its trust in its IMS.

For small operations, paper files may prove adequate to track and handle requests. For larger operations, it is essential to automate as

FIGURE 6. Cancellation Form

MEMO FROM: DOCUMENT DELIVERY

We have canceled this request because:

___This title is available in the Library. Please initiate a recall at the Circulation Desk

___We have contacted all available lenders and have been turned down.

___We are unable to locate or obtain the material with the information given. If you can provide us with additional information and would like for us to re-request the item, please notify us.

___This material was published so recently that it is not yet available for loan.

___This dissertation/thesis is not available for loan or purchase through Dissertation Express.

___This material does not circulate.

___We have canceled this request per your instructions.

___Other: _____

much of the ILL tracking process as possible to eliminate unneeded and redundant paper files.

Sample Paper Filing Setup

Pending

Use the Pending file for requests that have been submitted to potential suppliers. The easiest way to set up a pending file is to sort the requests in alphabetical order by patron name. Some libraries choose to further order requests by transaction number within each patron file.

Out-to-Patron

Use a second file for paperwork relating to materials on loan to patrons. This file can also be sorted by patron name, or it can be sorted by date due for easy retrieval of overdue items.

Completed

A third file can be used for storing completed requests again sorted by patron name. The file can be further divided into separate files: one for completed loans and one for completed photocopies. Most departments keep one year's worth of completed requests on file, usually until statistics are compiled. These older records may then be placed in file storage boxes and moved to a separate area of the department or library.

Records for completed photocopy requests must be kept in accordance with the CONTU Guidelines, though there are no record retention requirements for completed loan requests. Some libraries keep these files for one year, for three years, or for some other prescribed length of time.

Other Files

Depending upon the operation, some departments keep additional files of problem requests and/or cancellations. It is up to the individual departments to decide what additional files, if any, are required.

Some departments may also organize their workflow to have various "placeholder" files to hold requests as they are handled by staff. For example, a borrowing staff member may be ordering a batch of materials on OCLC, and encounter a request that is not listed in WorldCat. She may place that request in a Verification file that is checked periodically by the ILL librarian. She may also encounter requests that may be owned by the library and need to be checked against the library's OPAC. Departments may also use placeholder files when initially handling requests at the beginning of the workday.

Placeholder Files/Trays

Below is a sample list of some of the types of placeholder files that a department may wish to use:

- *Conditional*–This file/tray holds conditional messages sent by a potential supplier to the borrowing library. These conditional messages may indicate that the citation is incorrect, that the cost will exceed the library's stated maximum cost, or any other message that the borrowing library needs to address.
- *Unfilled*–This file/tray holds notifications that requests have gone unfilled. Many libraries store unfilled notices in a file until they can pull the corresponding original requests from the Pending file.
- *Renewal Requests*–This file/tray holds requests for renewals that need to be processed. Many libraries "batch process" a number of tasks during the ILL workday. Renewal requests are usually batch processed at the end of the day, along with other updates to pending requests.
- *Verification*–This file/tray holds requests that need further research/ verification before they can be submitted to a potential supplier.
- *Overdue*–This file/tray holds request forms, pulled from the Out-to-Patron file, that represent overdue materials.

Depending upon the individual departmental situation, the number and type of placeholder files will vary.

RECEIVING MATERIALS

Materials received by the borrowing group should be unpacked carefully and any damage should be noted immediately. According to the

National Interlibrary Loan Code, the borrowing library is responsible
for materials from the time they leave the lending library until the time
they arrive back at the lending library (2001, 4.8).

Keep any accompanying paperwork with the material, and pull the
matching request forms from the Pending file, or search each request in
your IMS and update the record to "Received." Ensure that the material
received matches the patron's request. If it does not, set the material and
paperwork aside for further investigation.

Most libraries receive multiple shipments during the day. The FedEx
courier may deliver at 10 a.m. followed by U.S. mail at 12 noon, followed by UPS at 12:30. Some libraries unpack materials immediately
as they arrive, while others wait and unpack materials after all deliveries
have been received for the day. It is an individual departmental choice,
based upon staff time, breakdown of the workday and other factors. Im-
plement whatever procedure is most efficient and contributes to getting
the material to patrons as fast as possible.

Materials (namely photocopies) may also be delivered to the department electronically, using ARIEL, for example. ARIEL is a software
package created by the Research Libraries Group (RLG) that transmits
and receives copies of scanned materials. These are usually printed out
and checked for quality. Again, the matching request form must be
pulled from a file or located on the IMS. After unpacking and matching,
a pile of material awaits the next step in the process: updating.

UPDATING REQUESTS

If the department is using an IMS, the updating step is often done at
the same time as receipt of the material. For paper-electronic hybrid
systems, departments may still need to "update" requests in an IMS.
These updates often are then transmitted to a bibliographic utility.

At this point in the process, libraries may also choose to annotate the
request forms (electronic or paper) with the date received, the name or
symbol of the supplying library, and any special conditions or restrictions on the use of the material.

PROCESSING MATERIALS

After updating, materials are then processed for patron use. This
usually includes placing a book strap or label on the borrowed item,

desensitizing materials (to avoid setting off the library's security alarms), moving materials to their pickup point and notifying patrons the material is ready.

Book Straps/Labels

Most ILL departments use a book strap placed on the borrowed material.

Be sure to note the following:

- Patron's name or ID number
- Date Due
- Any special restrictions on the use of the material, e.g., Library Use Only, No Photocopying, etc.

Some libraries, especially those using ILLiad, use a label (Avery 6464) that contains an adhesive similar to that found on a Post-it note. Many lending libraries use them on outgoing material sent to other libraries. Other libraries, however, do not use these labels and do not want borrowing libraries to place them on their materials. It is recommended that departments continue to use book straps for material borrowed from other libraries unless the lending library has indicated that the use of labels is permitted.

Alternatively, the library may modify the WORD® templates included with ILLiad to suit their own needs, be it a book strap, a label, or a single sheet of paper included with the material. (See Appendix E for samples of ILLiad WORD templates.)

To save additional processing time, some libraries will not place a book strap on a book that arrives with one already placed on it by the lending library. Often the book strap or label placed on the material by the lending library includes all of the pertinent information, such as the ILL transaction number and the patron's name. Borrowing libraries may annotate the existing book strap with additional information such as the location to return the material to and continue with processing.

In the final steps of processing, materials are moved to the area where patrons pick up ILL materials and the patron is notified that their material is available. More and more often, this is accomplished by e-mail, though some libraries continue to notify patrons by letter, postcard, or phone call.

The following is an example of an e-mail notification sent to patrons:

TO: lhilyer@rice.edu "Lee Andrew Hilyer"
FROM: ill@smithfield.edu "Interlibrary Borrowing "
RE: Your ILL Request
DATE: 30 October 2004

Dear Patron,

The material you requested through Interlibrary Borrowing has arrived and is available for pickup at the Circulation Desk, First Floor, Smithfield Library.

If you have any questions, please contact our office.

Sincerely,

Interlibrary Borrowing
ill@smithfield.edu

DELIVERY OF MATERIALS

Some departments will send materials directly to patrons (such as distance education students (see Chapter 7). Others will deliver materials via campus mail or delivery service, while some libraries will send only photocopies by campus mail, requiring patrons to pick up books and other loaned materials in person.

Other libraries deliver photocopies electronically, using software products such as Prospero, DocMorph, or version 3.0 of ARIEL.

RENEWAL REQUESTS

From time to time, patrons will want additional time to use materials. If the lending library has not prohibited renewals, update the request in the IMS to "Renewal Request" status and await the response from the lending library. If the item was not borrowed through a bibliographic utility or other automated method, borrowing staff will need to pull the paperwork and contact the library directly to request the renewal.

If the renewal is granted, the status of the request will change and a new due date will be provided. For example, when a library using OCLC answers affirmatively to a renewal request, the status changes to "Renewal OK." Notify the patron of the new due date, instructing him or her to write the new due date on the book strap.

For libraries that route ILL-borrowed materials through their circulation system, patrons may be able to automatically request and receive renewal information much as they do with the library's own materials.

RETURNING MATERIALS

When the patron is finished with the material, he will return it to the ILL office. Records will need to be updated (in the IMS, on OCLC, or RLIN) at this point to a "Returned" status. The department will also need to package materials securely for return to lending libraries. Many people do not like using "Jiffy" bags, preferring instead to use "bubble" mailers or cardboard boxes for packaging.

DAMAGED BOOKS

If materials come back damaged from patron use, it is best to discuss the matter with the patron when they return the material. If not, borrowing staff will need to contact the patron to determine the circumstances of the damage. Both libraries and patrons are responsible for the material. Most libraries will bill back to patrons any charges imposed by a lending library for damaged or lost materials.

PROBLEM-SOLVING

Problem solving occurs at every step of the Interlibrary Borrowing process. If possible, borrowing staff should set aside a portion of the workday to attend to problems, such as receipt of wrong material, missing pages from photocopies, unfilled requests, and overdue notices.

TECHNOLOGY

Look back at the daily timeline at the beginning of this chapter and examine all of the technology listed in it: ILLiad Connector, ILLiad, OCLC, DOCLINE, ARIEL, TIFF, PDF, and more. Technology is the key to today's faster ILL service and is essential to providing the high-quality library services that users have come to expect.

ILL Management Systems (IMS)

ILL management systems (IMS) such as VDX, Relais, and OCLC ILLiad are central to any high-performing ILL operation. Ranging in price from under $1,000 to over $5,000, an IMS is a database (such as Microsoft Access or SQL (Structured Query Language)) that helps a department electronically manage its ILL requests.

These types of systems usually offer a web-based interface to allow patrons to interact with the database, submitting requests for materials, checking status on requests, and retrieving electronic copies of materials. A staff interface is available for managing requests and usually enables interaction with related systems. For example, ILLiad users can access the OCLC ILL system directly through ILLiad's LiveLink, which is essentially a Passport client embedded within ILLiad.

ILL management systems save much of the time and effort involved with processing ILL requests. Because an electronic copy is involved, there is no tedious filing of paper requests, no rifling through folders to check status for a patron, and the time required to process a request is reduced to as little as one minute or less in some cases.

ILLiad Connector, mentioned in the timeline, is a batch program component that can be scheduled to run automatically to download and update requests to and from the OCLC ILL subsystem. Staff arriving early in the morning can immediately begin working on requests that were downloaded while they were still getting the morning paper off the lawn.

While ILL management systems can help achieve incredible efficiencies, their installation and administration can sometimes require expertise in a number of technological areas for anything other than simple changes. Customizing the web pages that comprise the ILLiad web patron interface requires knowledge of HTML, as well as basic familiarity with CGI scripts. If you are considering the purchase of an IMS, consult *Part II: Resources* for more information on selecting and implementing an IMS.

Bibliographic Utilities

OCLC ILL, DOCLINE, and RLG (RLIN) are the three most widely used bibliographic utilities. Bibliographic utilities are built on a central asset of bibliographic records, either for whole items (OCLC WorldCat, RLIN) or for articles (DOCLINE). OCLC has additional "subsystems" for cataloging, Interlibrary Loan, and resource discovery (OCLC FirstSearch). RLG has similar systems for the same functions (cataloging, ILL, and resource discovery). DOCLINE provides access to the National Library of Medicine's MEDLINE database of over 50 million medical literature citations.

OCLC ILL functions on a "whole item" level, meaning that libraries usually identify a record describing a single book or single journal title. Article-level materials (book chapters, tables of contents, journal articles) can be easily specified within a request, but a user must first search the database and identify that whole item before the "part" can be requested. DOCLINE by contrast, works on an article level. Users of the DOCLINE system use PubMed to search the MEDLINE database and identify the citation of the article requested. Incomplete citations or citations not found in the MEDLINE database can be manually requested and can also be built from a successful search in the library's catalog (LocatorPlus).

Delivery

Today's ILL department, like today's library, is a hybrid of print and electronic resources. Patrons are becoming more and more comfortable downloading their journal articles from the plethora of full-text databases and e-journals available. ILL articles should be as easily available.

ARIEL

In concert with their IMS, many libraries provide electronic delivery of requested articles through the use of ARIEL software, originally created by RLG and now owned by Infotrieve. ARIEL works with just about any scanner and uses multi-page TIFF format to scan and deliver materials to/from libraries. These received TIFF files can then be printed and processed manually, or they can be converted to PDF (Portable Document Format) and sent by e-mail or posted to a secure website for retrieval by the patron at their convenience. ARIEL itself offers a patron delivery module, making ARIEL a total solution for complete electronic delivery.

PROSPERO

Developed at the Prior Health Sciences Library in Ohio, Prospero is an open-source, absolutely free software package for electronic document delivery. It consists of a staff interface for managing and up-loading requests, and a web interface that allows patrons to securely access, view, and print their electronic documents. Prospero provides a few more bells and whistles than the ARIEL built-in patron delivery module, though it requires a bit of programming knowledge to install and administer.

There are those patrons who will continue to prefer alternate methods of delivery such as mail, pickup, and fax, but many ILL departments have found that their patrons embrace electronic delivery, and quickly migrate to it as their exclusive delivery method for photocopies.

Electronic Books (E-Books)

With the increased purchase and use of e-books in libraries has come a new dilemma for ILL departments: whether or not to request a print version of an item the library already owns electronically. In February 2004, the ILL-L listserv hosted a lengthy discussion of the issue. Opinions were varied on the issue as a whole, but generally fell into two camps: one sympathetic to the student due to the current state of e-book interfaces (page-by-page viewing; no ability to download chapters; no ability to print large portions of the text; difficulty using e-books for an extended period of time); and another camp arguing the issue from a "version" standpoint.

One librarian argued that their library does not use ILL for a regular print version of something if the large print version is available; likewise, they will not borrow print copies of material already held in microfiche.

E-book interfaces will continue to evolve and should eventually serve most users' needs. Until then, the ILL department should examine the issue locally and decide upon a course of action, preferably before the issue arises.

RESOURCES

Consult the Borrowing and Technology sections in *Part II: Resources* for an annotated list of materials for further information.

WORK CITED

Jackson, Mary E. 1998. Measuring the Performance of Interlibrary Loan Operations in North American Research and College Libraries. Washington, DC: Association of Research Libraries.

Chapter 4

Lending

SUMMARY. Lending to other libraries completes the ILL cycle. Chapter 4 includes a sample "daily timeline" of the activities of the lending section of an ILL department. Additional detailed information on managing the lending workflow is provided along with a sample lending policy document which lending libraries can use to provide uniform service to borrowing libraries. *[Article copies available for a fee from The Haworth Document Delivery Service: 1-800-HAWORTH. E-mail address: <docdelivery@haworthpress.com> Website: <http://www.HaworthPress.com> © 2006 by The Haworth Press, Inc. All rights reserved.]*

KEYWORDS. ILL lending, OCLC ILLiad, request forms, ILL management systems, daily routine

All libraries who request materials on behalf of their own patrons should help complete the ILL cycle by lending materials to requesting libraries.

SAMPLE DAILY TIMELINE

Accepting Requests

Many libraries have requirements on how they will accept requests (by DOCLINE® only, for example), or they may have special instruc-

---

[Haworth co-indexing entry note]: "Lending." Hilyer, Lee Andrew. Co-published simultaneously in *Journal of Interlibrary Loan, Document Delivery & Electronic Reserve* (The Haworth Information Press, an imprint of The Haworth Press, Inc.) Vol. 16, No. 1/2, 2006, pp. 41-51; and: *Interlibrary Loan and Document Delivery: Best Practices for Operating and Managing Interlibrary Loan Services in All Libraries* (Lee Andrew Hilyer) The Haworth Information Press, an imprint of The Haworth Press, Inc., 2006, pp. 41-51. Single or multiple copies of this article are available for a fee from The Haworth Document Delivery Service [1-800-HAWORTH, 9:00 a.m. - 5:00 p.m. (EST). E-mail address: docdelivery@haworthpress.com].

tions for expedited or unusual requests. The HAM-TMC Library, for example, requests that libraries in need of RUSH service place requests on OCLC or DOCLINE *first*, then fax a copy of the request to them for fulfillment. This is to ensure that they begin processing the request in as timely a manner as possible, as they currently download twice a day (once at 6 a.m.; again at 1 p.m.).

6:00 a.m.   ILLiad Connector program completes a scheduled download of the newest lending requests on the OCLC ILL subsystem as well as any updates to existing requests.

6:30 a.m.   Lending staff arrive and log in to their workstations.

Review Incoming Requests from Other Libraries

Generally, the lending group will start their workday by reviewing the new requests from other libraries that have come in overnight. Libraries currently using OCLC's ILL Microenhancer software to schedule batch processing (downloading or updating) will have to migrate to the FirstSearch platform by the summer of 2005. Procedures will vary, depending upon the bibliographic utility and ILL management system used by the department. No matter what type of system is used, initial processing of lending requests often concludes with a stack of printed forms used to retrieve items from the stacks and for updating.

6:45 a.m.   DOCLINE requests are downloaded and imported into ILLiad. Lending staff will generally then review the day's requests, checking for a number of potential factors:

- Who is this requesting library? Do we have a relationship (reciprocal agreement; consortial partner; other agreement) with this library?
- What do they want? A loan or a photocopy? Other special material?
- When do they need it? Is RUSH processing requested?
- How do they want the item delivered?
- How will we bill this library? By invoice? By monthly statement? By other method, such as OCLC ILL Fee Management (IFM)?

Much request review can be automated through the judicious use of grouping and "routing rules" in an ILL request management system such as RLG ILL Manager, Clio, or ILLiad.

Call Number Lookup

Once requests are initially reviewed, they are then searched in the library's catalog with call numbers and location information added for retrieval. Some ILL request management systems offer automatic Z39.50 searching of your local OPAC. In some systems, requests can be deflected automatically if the catalog indicates the item is missing or checked out to a library patron.

For most medical libraries, the workload usually consists of approximately 80-90% photocopy requests and 10-20% book or AV loan requests. Academic libraries, on the other hand, generally receive a larger amount of loan requests, making the OPAC searching capability a true timesaver.

If lending staff encounter any difficulties with a request at this stage of the process, they may pass those requests on to the ILL librarian for research/further review. The ILL librarian may choose to attempt to correct the citation error, or he/she may send a message to the requesting library, indicating the need for verification/research on the request.

7:00 a.m. Loansome Doc requests are downloaded manually and either printed for stacks retrieval or transferred to the DOCLINE system for fulfillment by another library.

7:30 a.m. Library Assistant arrives and retrieves the day's first batch of pick slips.

Retrieval

Reviewed requests are then sorted for retrieval from the stacks. If you have branch libraries, you may fax or hand-deliver the requests to those libraries. Requests for items from special departments in the library often require specific approval for loan to other libraries.

Students generally perform the bulk of retrieval services in ILL departments, though in some departments, staff also participates in the retrieval process.

While students are busy pulling materials from the stacks, other lending staff begin handling tasks such as renewal requests, special area requests, and updating materials that have been returned.

8:00 a.m.   Library Assistant arrives and begins scanning materials retrieved the previous afternoon.

All Day   Throughout the day, lending staff answer questions by phone or by e-mail to inquiries both from other libraries as well as the library's own patrons.

Lending staff may also produce overdue notices or process lost book invoices and may receive requests for RUSH service during the day. Depending on the type of services offered, lending staff might stop work on one part of the process to quickly retrieve and process the RUSH request. Other work to handle includes requests for re-sends of already delivered materials due to missing pages, poor quality, etc.

10:30 a.m.   Books and other materials to be loaned are prepared for shipping and updated on the ILLiad system.

Loan Processing

Once materials to be loaned have returned from the stacks, they need to be processed. For books and other returnables, this generally involves:

- "Updating" a request to "shipped" status in an IMS or directly on a bibliographic utility (OCLC, RLIN)
- Strapping/Labeling the book with pertinent ILL information
- Including the pick slip/request form with the material
- Checking materials out through the library's circulation system
- Packaging and delivery of materials through UPS, U.S. mail, FedEx, or other delivery method.

Copy Processing

Processing copies is much easier and quicker. Lending staff will update the request to "shipped" status and either scan the material for delivery via ARIEL or make photocopies for mail or fax delivery.

Billing

If any invoices have been created, these should be included with the material. If invoices are not readily available, or if libraries are invoiced on a monthly basis, charges should be noted on any paperwork sent to the borrowing library so that they may be aware of them and collect them from their patron if necessary.

If items are billed by OCLC's ILL Fee Management (IFM) service or EFTS (medical libraries equivalent of IFM), be sure that the borrowing library's Maxcost field indicates IFM, and that the corresponding Lending Charges field also includes IFM. Refer to the OCLC ILL Service User Guide for more information on IFM.

Delivery Methods

Package materials securely for safe delivery to the borrowing library. Use bubble mailers or cardboard boxes instead of used envelopes or "Jiffy" bags whenever possible. Insure valuable, fragile, or rare materials against loss or damage.

Depending on the circumstances, materials will probably be sent to borrowing libraries in a number of ways. For books, the most common methods in order of recommendation are:

- FedEx (Next-Day, 2nd-Day, and Ground)
- Private courier services (such as TExpress, the Texas statewide courier system)
- UPS (Ground and 2nd-Day Air)
- U.S. mail (Book or Library Rate, Media Mail, or First Class)

For copies and other non-returnables, the most common methods in order of preference are:

- ARIEL (Article or chapter is scanned and delivered via FTP)
- Fax
- E-mail or Web delivery
- U.S. mail (First Class preferred)
- Private courier services

Choose a delivery method that will ensure the material arrives at the borrowing library as quickly as possible within the budgetary constraints of the department.

12:30 p.m. ILLiad Connector program completes a scheduled download of the newest lending requests on the OCLC ILL subsystem as well as any updates to existing requests. Any morning requests already scanned and delivered to the requesting library are updated on the system.

1:00 p.m.   Lunchtime!

1:30 p.m.   Above cycle repeats (with daily variation).
Lending staff may also perform tasks such as producing overdue notices, processing lost book invoices, handling rush requests, or preparing an EFTS transfer file.

3:30 p.m.   Updates to any DOCLINE requests are uploaded to the system through ILLiad.
High-volume operations should consider investing in barcode scanners and using the barcodes included on DOCLINE and OCLC or ILLiad request pick slips. Using barcode scanners can help reduce processing time.

6:00 p.m.   ILLiad Connector program completes a scheduled update of any requests filled during the work day.

FILING

If the lending group uses an IMS, there is no need for paper files of any kind. Staff should rely on the data in their IMS and their circulation system to manage lending requests. Libraries who have achieved "paperless" lending simply include the pick slip/request form used in retrieval with the material shipped to the borrowing library. If this paperwork is returned with the item after the loan, it is simply discarded.

For loans from special collections, restricted loans, or other cases, files may be appropriate. However, if the data is contained within the IMS, the lending department should strive to rely on that data and not create additional and redundant paper files.

RENEWAL REQUESTS

Borrowing libraries will request renewals for the materials borrowed by their patrons. Whenever possible, accommodate renewal requests. This usually involves responding to a request whose status has changed to "Renewal Request" on OCLC, or to a phone call or e-mail from the library requesting the renewal. To simplify matters, try to make the renewal period as long as the original loan period. Update the request as necessary on the IMS or bibliographic utility, and notify the Circulation department so that the item may be renewed in the circulation system.

RETURNS

When materials are returned, book straps, labels, and any paperwork are removed. Materials are then checked for any damage, updated to "Completed" in the IMS or bibliographic utility, and sent to the Circulation department for discharge and return to the shelves.

OVERDUE ITEMS

Whenever possible, the library's circulation system or the department's IMS should handle the creation and delivery of overdue notices. Most IMS systems provide for the generation of overdue notices, and some will even e-mail the overdue notice to the borrowing library. If a paper file is in effect, check it periodically to identify overdue items and to prepare notices to send to the borrowing library.

INTERNATIONAL LENDING CONSIDERATIONS

Today, with increased access to faraway databases and resources, patrons more and more are requesting materials that are found only in foreign libraries. Today's ILL department needs to be able to borrow materials from libraries around the world, and they also need to be able to lend around the world.

Also, many libraries are hesitant about loaning their materials outside of the U.S. However, if the department requests materials from abroad, it should be willing to lend materials to other libraries outside of the U.S.

International lending requires some additional attention to detail and preparation, but it is easily accomplished. Provided the department takes some common-sense precautions and prepares adequate procedures, the library's books will be as safe overseas as they are here at home in the U.S.

INTERLIBRARY LENDING POLICY

In addition to a thorough borrowing policy, the department should also have a policy document available to libraries wishing to borrow from its library collections. Include the following sections of information in your department's lending policy:

Contact Information

Provide full contact information–mailing address, street address (for UPS and FedEx), phone numbers, fax numbers, e-mail addresses, ARIEL addresses, OCLC, RLIN, and NUC symbols–in short, everything that identifies the library. It is also often helpful to provide a link to the department's website if it offers information and forms for borrowing libraries.

Departments should also provide the URL for the library's catalog, as this will encourage borrowers to check the catalog and verify the ownership and disposition of an item before sending a request.

If certain staff members handle lending requests, borrowing libraries should be instructed to contact those staff members first when questions arise.

Affiliations/Memberships

If the library is a member of consortia or other groups that impact ILL service, be sure to list these in the lending policy. Also, be sure to note any specific courier or delivery instructions if necessary.

Federal Tax ID Number (FEIN)

Many libraries are not able to pay invoices without a Federal Tax ID number. Include it prominently in the lending policy document. *Note: Some institutions prefer not to publicize their FEIN, considering it a breach of security.* Consult with library administration or the Accounting department before including the FEIN in a lending policy.

Accepting Requests

Indicate the methods borrowing libraries may use to request materials from the library (OCLC, RLIN, DOCLINE, fax, e-mail, etc.). Be sure also to indicate any special requirements for RUSH service (i.e., place the request on OCLC, then fax a copy of the request, etc.).

Types of Materials

Indicate the types of materials available/unavailable through Interlibrary Loan. Most libraries highlight what they will not lend. This may include audiovisual materials, newspapers, microfilm, bound and unbound journals, etc., though departments are encouraged to be as liberal as possible in their lending policies. Departments should also note specifically what the policy is on dissertations and theses–often a difficult item to obtain via ILL, especially if they are not available from UMI.

Loan Period/Renewals

Indicate the loan period available, as well as the renewal period, if renewals are granted.

Charges/Fees

Indicate fees for ILL service as clearly as possible, preferably in table format.

Payment Methods

Indicate the payment methods available to borrowing libraries:

- Invoice
- OCLC ILL Fee Management (IFM) (If IFM is a preferred method of payment, is there a surcharge for non-IFM payment types, i.e., Invoice?)
- Credit Cards (which types?)
- IFLA vouchers
- Wire transfers
- Postage
- Other coupons or payment systems

Other Information

Include any other necessary information or information that would be helpful to borrowing libraries.

Distribution

Distribute a printed copy with all loaned materials on a periodic basis, perhaps once a year, or whenever substantial changes are made to the policy, such as a price increase or a new method of requesting. The policy should also be available on the Web whenever possible.

Also, the ILL supervisor should periodically check the department's OCLC ILL Policies Directory or other directory entries to ensure that borrowing libraries have the most up-to-date and accurate information available.

The following is a sample Lending Policy:

Interlibrary Loan
Rice University Library, MS-240

P.O. Box 1892   6100 Main St.
Houston, TX 77251-1892   Houston, TX 77005

713-348-3553 / Fax: 713-348-4117 / ill@rice.edu / OCLC: RCE
ARIEL 128.42.74.7 (or arieldoc@rice.edu)

Service Policy/Price List (Effective February 19, 2001)

PATRON	LOAN	PHOTOCOPY	International Payment Options
U.S. Libraries	$15.00	$15.00	
Canada/Mexico	$20.00	$15.00 ARIEL	Or **1.5 IFLA Vouchers**
		$20.00 MAIL	Or **2.0 IFLA Vouchers**
All Others	$30.00	$15.00 ARIEL	Or **1.5 IFLA Vouchers**
		$30.00 MAIL	Or **3 IFLA Vouchers**
Dissertations	$60.00 (purchase; foreign libraries only. U.S. libraries can purchase copies from UMI)		Or **6 IFLA Vouchers**

Rice now participates in IFM!
We also accept MasterCard, VISA and American Express.

Lending services are FREE to member libraries of the following groups:

HARLiC; TexShare; Big XII+; ARL (Free loans only); CARLA; Reciprocal Partners; Governmental Libraries (Some exceptions apply.)

Circulation of materials:

Some types of materials are generally not available through Interlibrary Loan. Please see our OCLC NAD record for more information. Call or e-mail the ILL Librarian if you have questions about a specific item.
Search our library catalog at: http://www-library.rice.edu

Loan periods:

All material is loaned out for <u>25 days</u> unless otherwise indicated. <u>One 25-day renewal</u> is granted unless the material is needed for use by one of the library's patrons.

For further information:

For further information or to discuss a reciprocal agreement, call Lee Andrew Hilyer, ILL Librarian, at 713-348-8837 or e-mail to lhilyer@rice.edu.

THANK YOU FOR USING INTERLIBRARY LOAN!

RESOURCES

Consult the Lending and Technology sections in *Part II: Resources* for further information. See also Appendix E for sample ILLiad Lending pick slips and other templates.

Chapter 5

Copyright
in the Interlibrary Loan Department

SUMMARY. All members of the Interlibrary Loan department need to be aware of current copyright law and related guidelines. Within the past ten years, there have been significant changes to the copyright laws (Sonny Bono Copyright Term Extension Act, Digital Millennium Copyright Act, TEACH Act, etc.), which have had an impact on the provision of library services, including ILL. Chapter 5 provides extensive background on the provisions of copyright law applicable to interlibrary loan, and also provides practical examples of how those laws and regulations are applied on a daily basis within the ILL department. *[Article copies available for a fee from The Haworth Document Delivery Service: 1-800-HAWORTH. E-mail address: <docdelivery@haworthpress.com> Website: <http://www.HaworthPress.com> © 2006 by The Haworth Press, Inc. All rights reserved.]*

KEYWORDS. Copyright, fair use, CONTU Guidelines, public domain, copyright compliance

INTRODUCTION

As with the other codes and regulations discussed in Chapter 2, all members of the Interlibrary Loan department need to be aware of cur-

[Haworth co-indexing entry note]: "Copyright in the Interlibrary Loan Department." Hilyer, Lee Andrew. Co-published simultaneously in *Journal of Interlibrary Loan, Document Delivery & Electronic Reserve* (The Haworth Information Press, an imprint of The Haworth Press, Inc.) Vol. 16, No. 1/2, 2006, pp. 53-64; and: *Interlibrary Loan and Document Delivery: Best Practices for Operating and Managing Interlibrary Loan Services in All Libraries* (Lee Andrew Hilyer) The Haworth Information Press, an imprint of The Haworth Press, Inc., 2006, pp. 53-64. Single or multiple copies of this article are available for a fee from The Haworth Document Delivery Service [1-800-HAWORTH, 9:00 a.m. - 5:00 p.m. (EST). E-mail address: docdelivery@haworthpress.com].

rent copyright law and related guidelines. Within the past ten years, there have been significant changes to the copyright laws (Sonny Bono Copyright Term Extension Act, Digital Millennium Copyright Act, TEACH Act, etc.), which have had an impact on the provision of library services, including ILL.

Copyright is a complex topic that cannot be easily covered in a single chapter, yet an extensive knowledge of every nuance of copyright law is not required for successful (and legal) operation of an ILL department. This chapter will acquaint those new to ILL with the fundamentals of copyright with specific guidelines for ILL.

Bear in mind however, that the author is not a lawyer, and the information presented in this chapter should not be construed as legal advice. Consult with your library administration and/or institutional counsel before setting departmental policies.

WHAT IS COPYRIGHT?

Copyright is a form of protection provided by the laws of the United States (title 17, U.S. Code) to the authors of "original works of authorship" including literary, dramatic, musical, artistic, and certain other intellectual works [books, journal articles, musical compositions, etc.]. This protection is available to both published and unpublished works. Section 106 of the 1976 Copyright Act generally gives the owner of copyright the exclusive right to do and to authorize others to do the following:

To reproduce the copyrighted work in copies or phonorecords;

To prepare derivative works based upon the copyrighted work;

To distribute copies or phonorecords of the copyrighted work to the public by sale or other transfer of ownership, or by rental, lease, or lending;

To perform the copyrighted work publicly, in the case of literary, musical, dramatic, and choreographic works, pantomimes, and motion pictures and other audiovisual works;

To display the copyrighted work publicly, in the case of literary, musical, dramatic, and choreographic works, pantomimes, and pictorial, graphic, or sculptural works, including the individual images of a motion picture or other audiovisual work; and

In the case of *sound recordings, to perform the work publicly* by means of a *digital audio transmission.*

In addition, certain authors of works of visual art have the rights of attribution and integrity as described in section 106A of the 1976 Copyright Act. For further information, request Circular 40, "Copyright Registration for Works of the Visual Arts."

It is illegal for anyone to violate any of the rights provided by the copyright code to the owner of copyright. These rights, however, are not unlimited in scope. Sections 107 through 120 of the 1976 Copyright Act establish limitations on these rights. In some cases, these limitations are specified exemptions from copyright liability. *One major limitation is the doctrine of "fair use," which is given a statutory basis in section 107 of the 1976 Copyright Act.* In other instances, the limitation takes the form of a "compulsory license" under which certain limited uses of copyrighted works are permitted upon payment of specified royalties and compliance with statutory conditions. For further information about the limitations of any of these rights, consult the copyright code or write to the Copyright Office (U.S. Copyright Office 2000).

DURATION OF COPYRIGHT

As set forth in the Sonny Bono Copyright Term Extension Act (PL105-298, 112 Stat. 2827 (1998)), items copyrighted after January 1, 1978 are now generally protected for the life of the copyright owner plus seventy years. Items published prior to January 1, 1978; enjoy a period of copyright protection that may vary from the current life-plus-seventy period (Gasaway, 2003).

Public Domain

When a copyright expires, or copyright protection is not requested or claimed, a work is said to be in the public domain, and is free from any restrictions on its use. For day-to-day use in the ILL department, a general rule-of-thumb is: If the item was first published more than ninety-five years ago, it is fairly safe to assume it is in the public domain, though some exceptions may apply. Departments can also consult Gasaway's chart <http://www.unc.edu/~unclng/public-d.htm> on when works pass into the public domain. If there is any doubt, consult with your library's or institution's legal counsel.

WHAT IS "FAIR USE"?

The doctrine of "fair use" is codified in Section 107 of Title 17 of the United States Code. Fair use helps to ensure that copyright serves its constitutional purpose ". . . to promote the progress of Science and Useful Arts" (U.S. Constitution, art. I, sec. 8, cl. 8). The doctrine of fair use permits teachers, librarians, students, and researchers to make reasonable uses of copyrighted materials without obtaining permission of the author or copyright-holder. A student's requests for copies of journal articles or book chapters are usually considered "fair uses" of copyrighted material since they are intended primarily for educational or research purposes.

> Notwithstanding the provisions of sections 106 and 106A, the fair use of a copyrighted work, including such use by reproduction in copies or phonorecords or by any other means specified in that section, for purposes such as criticism, comment, news reporting, teaching (including multiple copies for classroom use), scholarship, or research, is not an infringement of copyright.

> In determining whether the use made of a work in any particular case is a fair use the factors to be considered shall include–

> 1. The purpose and character of the use, including whether such use is of a commercial nature or is for nonprofit educational purposes;
> 2. The nature of the copyrighted work;
> 3. The amount and substantiality of the portion used in relation to the copyrighted work as a whole; and
> 4. The effect of the use upon the potential market for or value of the copyrighted work.

> The fact that a work is unpublished shall not itself bar a finding of fair use if such finding is made upon consideration of all the above factors. (U.S. Code, title 17, sec. 107)

A "defense" against copyright infringement, fair use permits students and faculty to make reasonable use of copyrighted materials (copies of articles, book chapters, etc.) for their own private use. The four items in the U.S. Code listed earlier are known as the "four factors." These are the factors that are examined when determining whether or not a copy is fair use of the copyrighted material.

SECTION 108 OF THE COPYRIGHT ACT: LIMITATIONS ON EXCLUSIVE RIGHTS: REPRODUCTION BY LIBRARIES AND ARCHIVES

Day-to-day services of the ILL department are covered in Section 108 of Title 17, and by the CONTU Guidelines. Sections 108(d) and (e) permit libraries to receive copies of copyrighted materials provided that two conditions are met: (1) the copy requested must become the property of the patron; and (2) the library must prominently display the "Copyright Warning," both at the place where requests are made and on the order form itself:

NOTICE: WARNING CONCERNING COPYRIGHT RESTRICTIONS

The copyright law of the United States (Title 17, United States Code) governs the making of photocopies or other reproductions of copyrighted material.

Under certain conditions specified in the law, libraries and archives are authorized to furnish a photocopy or other reproduction. One of these specific conditions is that the photocopy or reproduction is not to be "used for any purpose other than private study, scholarship or research." If a user makes a request for, or later uses, a photocopy or reproduction for purposes in excess of "fair use," that user may be liable for copyright infringement.

This institution reserves the right to refuse a copying order if, in its judgment, fulfillment of the order would involve violation of copyright law.

Section 108(g)(2) of the Code also prohibits systematic reproduction or distribution of ". . .aggregate quantities [of copies that would] substitute for a subscription to or purchase of [the] work." Section 108 of the Code does not specify the amount of copies that would be considered "aggregate," and as a result, the CONTU Guidelines were developed.

CONTU GUIDELINES

To address the issue of "aggregate quantities," among others, Congress formed the National Commission on New Technological Uses of Copyrighted Works (CONTU) while the Copyright Act was under consideration. This commission developed what is commonly known as the "Guideline of Five," or sometimes, the "Suggestion of Five."

> During *one* calendar year, no more than *five* copies may be received from any *one* work whose publication date is within *five* years of the date of the patron's request.

It is a standard five-year period from the date of the patron's request, so if a patron requested an item on January 1, 2004, the time period allowed for that journal title would extend back to January 1, 1999.

Example

January 1, 2004

Patron A requests the following articles:

Belis, Melissia. "Solving Group Conflict Issues: A Mediated Approach." *Journal of Social Work*. Volume 23, Number 4. *October 1999*. PP: 437-456.

White, David. "Career Objectives of Public Support Recipients." *Journal of Social Work*. Volume 23, Number 1. *January 1999*. PP: 23-45.

White, Anjeanette. "New Strategies in Domestic Abuse Counseling & Prevention." *Journal of Social Work*. Volume 25, Number 3. *August 2001*. PP: 3-18.

At this time, the department has requested and received three articles from the *Journal of Social Work*. The department may obtain two additional copies as permitted by the CONTU Guidelines.

March 12, 2004

Patron A returns and requests another article:

Lotz, Elizabeth. "Funding Sources for Social Services." *Journal of Social Work*. Volume 25, Number 2. *April 2001*. PP: 89-94.

Patron B requests the following article:

Belis, Melissia. "Solving Group Conflict Issues: A Mediated Approach." *Journal of Social Work*. Volume 23, Number 4. *October 1999*. PP: 437-456.

At this point, the department has now requested and received five articles. Patron B returns the next day and requests the following article:

Belis, Gene E. "Domestic Abuse Prevention: A Literature Review" *Journal of Social Work*. Volume 26, Number 1. *January 2002*. PP: 31-35.

The request above is the sixth for this journal title. To remain in compliance with copyright law and the CONTU Guidelines, there are numerous options available, which include:

- Refusing to request the copy and cancel the request;
- Attempting to borrow the journal issue needed;
- Requesting permission from the copyright holder;
- Sending the patron to a local library that owns a copy of the needed item;
- Obtaining a copy and paying the appropriate royalty for the additional copy in excess of the five permitted.

Many ILL management systems offer detailed tracking reports that can assist the department with its copyright compliance. Clio and ILLiad both provide a report of journal titles and counts of articles requested over the five allowed by the CONTU Guidelines. ILLiad also offers a web link to the Copyright Clearance Center for those libraries wishing to pay copyright as the need arises. Other libraries choose to pay their copyright compliance on a monthly, quarterly, yearly, or other periodic basis.

COPYRIGHT AND PUBLISHERS

Copyright protects "inventors" of literary and artistic works, much like a patent protects inventors of mechanical and chemical devices and processes. However, "inventors" such as university professors and researchers often transfer to the publishers the rights to their work once an article or manuscript has been accepted for publication. Most ILL copyright compliance issues will thus deal with publishers and not with individual authors as copyright-holders.

COPYRIGHT CLEARANCE CENTER (CCC)

One method for paying copyright royalties is to use the services of the Copyright Clearance Center (CCC). The CCC is a Reproduction Rights Organization (RRO) that acts as a broker between copyright holders and users of copyrighted materials. The CCC collects royalties on copyrighted materials from libraries and other users that are then paid to the owners of the copyrighted material.

The CCC offers a wide range of services, from copyright clearance for electronic reserves to classroom course packs and volume licensing. The service used by ILL departments is known as the Transactional Reporting Service (TRS). CCC users can access a database of copyright royalty pricing and information, and are able to report their copying in excess of amounts permitted by Section 108 and the CONTU Guidelines. The CCC then invoices the library or department for royalty payments due.

ITEMS OLDER THAN FIVE YEARS

The CONTU Commission did not address items published prior to five years from the date of the patron request. Because no guidelines were developed, ILL departments may consider requests for articles published more than five years from the date of the patron request to fall under Section 107.

REQUESTING ITEMS OWNED BY YOUR LIBRARY

If a patron requests materials owned by the library but currently unavailable to the patron, the department may order article copies which do not count against the "Guideline of Five," as the law considers the department to be making copies from the library's own collection. This is also true if the material is on order, but has not yet arrived.

Example

Patron A wants a copy of an article from the June 2003 issue of the *Journal of the American Chemical Society*. The library has a subscription to that journal, but the 2003 issues have been sent to the bindery. ILL may obtain a copy of the requested article that will not count against the five copies allowed each calendar year. This is because the library owns the journal, but the particular issue needed is unavailable.

INDICATING COPYRIGHT COMPLIANCE

When submitting requests for reproductions to other libraries, copyright compliance must be indicated on the form used for the request, be it a paper ALA form or an electronic one. There are two options for indicating copyright compliance:

1. CCG–"Conforms to CONTU Guidelines." The submitted request follows one of the CONTU Guidelines (see earlier).
2. CCL–"Conforms to [other provisions] of Copyright Law." While the request may not be permitted under CONTU Guidelines, it conforms to other provisions of the copyright law such as section 107 (the "fair use " section). "CCL" can be used for requests for copies from materials published earlier than the five-year period permitted in the CONTU Guidelines. *Note: Many libraries also use "CCL" to indicate requests for which they are paying royalties.*

The first five copies from a journal title requested and received in a calendar year (as described in the CONTU Guidelines) should indicate "CCG," since those requests "Conform to Copyright Guidelines." The sixth request from the journal title should include either "CCG" or "CCL," depending on how the department will consider that request.

COPYRIGHT CONSIDERATIONS FOR LENDING

While the requesting (borrowing) library is responsible for indicating copyright compliance on its requests, the lending library also has two responsibilities with regard to copyright. First, it needs to check that the ILL request includes an indication of copyright compliance (either "CCG" or "CCL"), and second, it needs to ensure that the copies it provides include a notice of copyright.

With the enactment of the Digital Millennium Copyright Act, the requirements for notice of copyright have changed. Previously, all that was required was the use of a stamp or label indicating:

Copyright Notice for Materials

"NOTICE: THIS MATERIAL MAY BE PROTECTED BY COPYRIGHT LAW (TITLE 17 U.S.C.)."

Now, however, the lending library is responsible for providing the original notice of copyright if it is included on the piece being copied, such as the journal article or book chapter. If the original notice is not available, stamping the article with the above-mentioned text is sufficient.

RETENTION OF REQUEST FORMS

For borrowing, the current calendar year's records, plus the previous three calendar years' records of filled requests are required by the CONTU Guidelines. This requirement only applies to requests for copies or reproductions and not to loan requests. Electronic request records should be purged from the IMS on the same schedule.

COPYING ENTIRE COPYRIGHTED WORKS

Copyright law generally prohibits the photocopying/reproduction of entire copyrighted works. However, there are occasional situations when it is permissible to request a photocopy of an entire work, usually if the intent is to replace a lost or damaged item.

Section 108(c) of the Copyright Act requires that a "reasonable effort" first be made to obtain a replacement copy at a "fair price." Sections

108(e) and (g) provide additional guidance when requesting copies of entire works. The provisions of Sections 108(c), (e), and (g) apply equally to copies of books and of journal articles, as no distinction is made in the law itself (see also: Boucher 1997, 204-205).

ELECTRONIC RESOURCE LICENSING AND INTERLIBRARY LOAN

Today, the Interlibrary Loan department both requests and provides copies that are increasingly obtained from electronic resources. However, because many of these electronic products are licensed and not owned by the library, use of these resources for ILL activity may be prohibited by the license agreement.

Departments must be careful when providing copies from electronic resources. ILL supervisors should read license agreements to determine if they can use the electronic resource to fill requests. Determining which electronic resource may be used to fill lending requests may prove challenging as other departments in the library often maintain the records for these resources. The task can be somewhat easier if a large portion of electronic journals come from one publisher or vendor. JSTOR <http://www.jstor.org>, for example, permits ILL as part of its license agreement, and provides access to several hundred journal titles. Individual ILL departments should consult with whoever maintains the license to determine if an electronic resource may be used to fill lending requests.

Libraries should try to ensure that license agreements for electronic resources contain language that permits their ILL departments to use the material to provide copies to other libraries. There is a risk that restrictive licensing agreements will have a detrimental effect on the availability of some resources, particularly electronic ones, since at present, licenses generally cover electronic and not print resources.

As more and more items become available electronically, libraries may cancel print subscriptions, and when a patron needs an item, libraries may have a more difficult time obtaining the material via ILL because providing copies from the electronic resource may be restricted, if not completely prohibited.

ILL departments have become active in looking for an equitable and comfortable solution for both the ILL department and the publisher when considering ILL from electronic resources. Yale University Library's LIBLICENSE project, is a website that collects information from publishers on the ILL provisions of their license agreements. The goal is to provide a quick reference resource ILL departments can use to determine if ILL is permitted from a particular e-journal or e-book.

RESOURCES

Consult the Copyright section in *Part II: Resources* for additional readings, websites, and other materials on Copyright in the ILL department.

WORKS CITED

Boucher, Virginia. 1997. Interlibrary Loan Practices Handbook. 2nd ed. Chicago: American Library Association.

Copyright Act of 1976. § 107, 17 U.S.C. (1976).

Gasaway, Laura. 2003. "When U.S. Works Pass into the Public Domain." <http://www.unc.edu/~unclng/public-d.htm>.

United States Copyright Office. 2000. Copyright Basics (Circular 1). <http://www.copyright.gov/circs/circ1.html>.

Chapter 6

Management of the Interlibrary Loan Department

SUMMARY. Many new ILL department heads are often new to supervision, and in addition to the challenges of managing a busy ILL service, new managers must also learn how to best supervise their most valuable resource–their staff. Supervising others can be one of the most daunting tasks a librarian has to face. Real-world strategies for hiring, motivating, and evaluating talented staff are discussed, along with practical guidance on budgeting, determining ILL costs, and quantitatively measuring ILL activity. *[Article copies available for a fee from The Haworth Document Delivery Service: 1-800-HAWORTH. E-mail address: <docdelivery@haworthpress.com> Website: <http://www.HaworthPress.com> © 2006 by The Haworth Press, Inc. All rights reserved.]*

KEYWORDS. Management, HR, human resources, hiring, evaluation, statistics, measurement, upward appraisal

HUMAN RESOURCES

First-Time Manager

Many new ILL department heads are new to supervision, and in addition to the challenges of managing a busy ILL service, new managers

[Haworth co-indexing entry note]: "Management of the Interlibrary Loan Department." Hilyer, Lee Andrew. Co-published simultaneously in *Journal of Interlibrary Loan, Document Delivery & Electronic Reserve* (The Haworth Information Press, an imprint of The Haworth Press, Inc.) Vol. 16, No. 1/2, 2006, pp. 65-74; and: *Interlibrary Loan and Document Delivery: Best Practices for Operating and Managing Interlibrary Loan Services in All Libraries* (Lee Andrew Hilyer) The Haworth Information Press, an imprint of The Haworth Press, Inc., 2006, pp. 65-74. Single or multiple copies of this article are available for a fee from The Haworth Document Delivery Service [1-800-HAWORTH, 9:00 a.m. - 5:00 p.m. (EST). E-mail address: docdelivery@haworthpress.com].

http://www.haworthpress.com/web/JILDD
© 2006 by The Haworth Press, Inc. All rights reserved.
doi:10.1300/J474v16n01_06

must also learn how to best supervise their most valuable resource–their staff. Supervising others can be one of the most daunting tasks a librarian has to face. Supervising is as much an art as a skill, and there are many excellent librarians who do not make good supervisors. Those already gifted with this type of talent should consider themselves lucky, while those who do not should be prepared to work at developing the skills and empathy required for effective supervision.

For new supervisors, one first step in establishing a solid relationship with your staff could be scheduling one-on-one interviews to allow staff members to answer a series of open-ended questions about what they do, what they enjoy about their work, and what the existing difficulties are that you and your staff will face. Be sure to listen carefully to their responses and avoid interrupting their answers. Consider their perceptions of the department's goals and mission and the library's or parent institution's mission and compare them with your own expectations.

Another recommendation is to spend your initial time with your new department observing, asking questions, reading departmental procedures and other relevant documents. Spend time "shadowing" each employee in your department to learn about their daily activities and how the current request workflow is managed. Every ILL supervisor should know how to perform the entire job operations of his/her staff to ensure backup coverage in case of absence as well as to be able to better plan for changes and improvements to the workflow, resulting in better service to the patron.

Be proactive with human resources–get to know your HR department and utilize their expertise and helpful suggestions to ensure a smooth initiation into a supervisory role. Keep detailed records of all of your human resources issues–absence reports, compliments, and complaints (from patrons or other staff), disciplinary actions, and any other paperwork relating to employees. Remember that employee information is *confidential* and should be kept secure at all times. If you encounter difficulties in your department, consider the HR department your primary resource to help you resolve the issue.

Hiring

In addition to the standard considerations of job applicants, ILL departments should consider posing the following additional questions:

Is this applicant. . .

- Able to recognize and identify the parts of a bibliographic citation?
- Able to use an article index to locate an article?
- Able to search the library catalog for both books and journals?
- Able to identify when there is "enough" information to send a request to a lender?
- Able to effectively search for materials in OCLC, DOCLINE®, and/or RLIN?

Employee Evaluation

In many libraries there is an annual program of evaluation for employees. This is a time for supervisors to recognize and reward good performance, and to coach an employee having difficulties or falling behind in some areas back to success.

One of the most useful tools that any supervisor can employ is the *upward appraisal*. The upward appraisal permits employees to anonymously rate their supervisor on a wide array of characteristics and skills such as fairness, problem-solving, and empathy. Additionally, employees appreciate the chance to provide feedback (both positive and negative) to their supervisor without any fear of repercussions.

Each August, employees of the HAM-TMC Library ILL department receive an upward appraisal form which they complete and return to the Director of Library Operations (who is the ILL librarian's supervisor). Responses are collated and the supervisor is presented with an anonymous report including the averages in each category. The ILL supervisor works with the Director to examine the results and identify strengths and areas for improvement.

Figure 1 is a sample upward appraisal form.

FIGURE 1. Sample Upward Appraisal Form for Supervisors

SUPERVISOR APPRAISAL

FOR:_____ PERIOD: _____

Instructions:

Below are a series of statements that are designed to help you evaluate your supervisor.

For each statement, use the scale listed below, marking each statement accordingly with the number that you think best reflects your judgment of your supervisor's performance.

Feelings about a supervisor may change from day to day, but for each statement, try to determine what your general attitude is toward your supervisor over the review period.

FIGURE 1 (continued)

Scale:

1	2	3	4	5
Needs substantial improvement	Below average	Average	Above Average	Excellent

GENERAL	
Provides effective leadership to the staff	
Serves as a good role model	
Sets a positive tone in the workplace	
Builds a spirit of teamwork among staff	
Provides constructive criticism to improve my work	
Responds to problems and/or suggestions in a timely manner	
Sets clear goals for the department	
Treats me courteously and with respect	
Is willing to implement new ideas proposed by staff	
Effectively resolves conflicts between staff members	
Deals effectively with inappropriate behavior of other staff members	
Is knowledgeable about the work in the department	
Provides the proper amount of supervision	
Handles emergencies in a calm and rational manner	
Is willing to delegate authority and responsibilities	
Recognizes my work when I perform well	
Conducts regular staff meetings as required	
Interprets library policies and rules accurately	
Gives clear explanations for infractions of library rules or policies	
COMMUNICATION	
Takes criticism from staff constructively	
Encourages staff opinions	
Communicates in a straightforward fashion with staff	
Is willing to listen to new ideas	
Uses tact when dealing with staff	
Keeps me informed in a timely manner about new decisions or policies	
FAIRNESS	
Treats employees fairly	
Is fair in the scheduling of vacation and holiday time	
Has reasonable work expectations for me	
Distributes work assignments fairly	
Enforces rules and policies fairly	

SUPPORT	
Works with staff to find solutions for problems	
Represents the interests of staff to administration	
Is approachable when I have a problem or concern	
Encourages any questions I may have about work	
Shows sufficient concern for the physical safety of staff	
Will personally assist staff when department gets busy	
Is a good source of information when I need assistance in my work	
Provides the necessary training for me to do my job well	
Backs me up when patrons challenge my decisions	
Gives me the freedom necessary to perform my job well	
Demonstrates confidence in my decisions	

Overall Assessment

Please indicate your overall evaluation of your supervisor by selecting the most appropriate description of your supervisor's performance from the statements below (select only one):

___My supervisor's performance is excellent (5).

___My supervisor's performance is above-average (4).

___My supervisor's performance is average (3).

___My supervisor's performance is below average (2).

___My supervisor's performance needs substantial improvement (1).

For any additional comments, please use a separate sheet of paper.

Figure 2 is a sample of aggregate scores from the appraisal process.

FIGURE 2. Upward Appraisal Score Sheet

Supervisor:　　　　Year:	A	B	C	D	E	F	Score
GENERAL							
Provides effective leadership to the staff	3	4	4	4	3	3	4
Serves as a good role model	3	5	4	4	3	3	4
Sets a positive tone in the workplace	3	5	4	3	3	4	4
Builds a spirit of teamwork among staff	1	5	3	4	3	3	3
Provides constructive criticism to improve my work	3	5	4	3	3	3	4
Responds to problems and/or suggestions in a timely manner	3	4	4	3	3	3	3
Sets clear goals for the department	4	3	5	4	4	3	4

FIGURE 2 (continued)

Supervisor: Year:	A	B	C	D	E	F	Score
GENERAL							
Treats me courteously and with respect	4	5	5	5	4	3	4
Is willing to implement new ideas proposed by staff	3	4	5	4	3	3	4
Effectively resolves conflicts between staff members	2	4	4	3	2	3	3
Deals effectively with inappropriate behavior of other staff members	1	4	4	3	3	3	0
Is knowledgeable about the work in the department	3	4	4	5	4	4	4
Conducts regular staff meetings as required	4	5	5	5	4	4	5
Provides the proper amount of supervision	3	5	4	3	1	3	3
Handles emergencies in a calm and rational manner	4	5	4	4	3	3	4
Is willing to delegate authority and responsibilities	3	3	4	3	3	3	3
Recognizes my work when I perform well	3	3	5	3	4	3	4
Conducts regular staff meetings as required	4	4	4	5	4		4
Interprets library policies and rules accurately	3	3	4	4	2	3	3
Give clear explanation for infractions of library rules or policies	3	4	5	4	2	3	4
COMMUNICATION							
Takes criticism from staff constructively	3	4	4	3	2	3	3
Encourages staff opinions	3	4	5	3	3	4	4
Communicates in a straightforward fashion with staff	3	5	4	3	3	4	4
Is willing to listen to new ideas	3	5	4	4	4	4	4
Uses tact when dealing with staff	3	4	4	4	3	3	4
Keeps me informed in a timely manner about new decisions or policies	5	5	5	4	3	3	4
FAIRNESS							
Treats employees fairly	2	5	5	4	3	3	4
Is fair in the scheduling of vaction and holiday time	3	4	5	3	3	4	4
Has reasonable work expectations for me	3	4	5	3	4	4	4
Distributes work assignments fairly	1	5	5	3	1	4	3
Enforces rules and policies fairly	1	4	5	3	1	3	3
SUPPORT							
Works with staff to find solutions for problems	3	4	5	3	4	4	4
Represents the interests of staff to administration	3	4	5	4	3	3	4

Is approachable when I have a problem or concern	3	5	5	5	4	3	4
Encourages any questions I may have about work	3	5	5	5	3	3	4
Show sufficient concern for the physical safety of staff	3	5	5	5	3	3	4
Will personally assist staff when department gets busy	3	5	5	5	3	4	4
Is a good source of information when I need assistance in my work	3	5	5	5	3	3	4
Provides the necessary training for me to do my job well	3	5	5	4	3	3	4
Backs me up when patrons challenge my decisions	3	4	5	4	3	3	4
Gives me the freedom necessary to perform my job well	3	5	5	5	3	3	4
Demonstrates confidence in my decisions	3	4	5	5	3	3	4
Overall Assessment	3	5	4	4	3	3	4

BUDGETING

Many ILL departments run under a separate budget and the ILL librarian must be capable of managing a budget from year to year. Forecasting is essential to provide the most accurate budget estimates and to minimize the gap between expected and actual revenues and expenses.

COSTING

It is often helpful to analyze Interlibrary Loan transaction costs in detail and there are a number of excellent articles and worksheets available. Costing is helpful in serving as a starting point for analyzing ILL activities with respect to the bottom line costs of doing so.

In medical libraries, where fees are often charged for ILL, the need for a structured analysis of expenses can help explain a fee structure, as well as justify price increases when necessary.

What are the costs of running an ILL department? Direct costs may include the fees libraries and commercial document suppliers charge for their services. Indirect costs include staff time, fringe benefits, postage, supplies, equipment, computer hardware and software, as well as "overhead" expenses such as electricity, rent, and telephone/Internet service.

QUANTITATIVE MEASUREMENT (STATISTICS)

Statistics are necessary in Interlibrary Loan, not only to measure past activity, but also to identify trends in usage (i.e., graduate student ILL activity is rising, but faculty use is falling–What are some of the reasons why?).

Statistics are also helpful in justifying changes to policies or procedures, or to justify additional funding. The "numbers" are what many administrators are interested in, and ILL supervisors must quantitatively evaluate a service or change in procedure to prove that it is/is not necessary.

The size and scope of statistics gathered in ILL departments varies greatly. The department may collect only basic statistics, while another may be required to provide detailed statistics not only to the administration, but to its consortial leadership as well.

Medical libraries, for example, often report statistics to the American Association of Health Sciences Libraries (AAHSL), as well as to institutional authorities within the healthcare system of which they are a member. Below is an example of a basic ILL borrowing statistical report:

BORROWING	02-03	03-04	% Change
Requests Rec'd	10012	12194	**21.79%**
Photocopies	4227	5768	**36.46%**
Book Loans	3463	3521	**1.67%**
Total Filled	7690	9289	**20.79%**
Unfilled	2322	2905	**25.11%**
Fill Rate (%)	76.81	76.18	***-0.63%***
In-State			
Book Loans	1860	1857	-0.16%
Photocopies	2964	3729	25.81%
Total In-State	4824	5586	15.80%
Out-of-State			
Book Loans	1597	1664	04.20%
Photocopies	1269	2039	60.68%
Total Out-of-State	2866	3703	29.20%

Comparative statistics often provide useful information for identification of trends and to quantitatively determine whether or not goals/objectives were met. From these statistics, it is evident that this department experienced a 22% increase in overall activity (total requests received) from one fiscal year to the next. This department's fill rate went down slightly (-0.63%) which is probably attributable to statistical error. However, if one of this department's goals was to improve fill rate, the numbers demonstrate that this goal was not met.

Supervisors should judiciously use statistics to learn more about their operations, and to set quantitative goals for their departments. For example, the supervisor of the above Interlibrary Loan department might set the goal of achieving an 85% fill rate for fiscal year 2004-2005. This would be a 9% increase over the 2003-2004 fiscal year. In consultation with borrowing staff members, the supervisor could identify areas of improvement that might lead to an increased fill rate.

Quantitative improvements often lead to qualitative ones. In our above example, we set a goal of achieving an 85% fill rate. This could be linked to a customer satisfaction survey that seeks information about patrons' perspectives on the amount of materials filled/unfilled that they request. Similarly, a quantitative goal to reduce turnaround time by one day would likely lead to increased patron satisfaction with the ILL service, since patrons would be receiving their materials one day earlier (if the quantitative goal were met).

Below are some statistics on Interlibrary Lending activities for the same department:

LENDING	98-99	99-00	% Change
Requests Rec'd	16725	18673	**11.65%**
Photocopies	2493	2640	**05.90%**
Book Loans	6804	8135	**19.56%**
Total Filled	9297	10775	**15.90%**
Unfilled	7428	7898	**06.33%**
Fill Rate (%)	55.59	57.70	**02.12%**
In-State			
Book Loans	3843	4430	15.27%
Photocopies	1169	1119	−4.28%
Subtotal	5012	5549	10.71%
Unfilled	3012	3111	03.29%
Total In-State	8024	8660	10.71%
Out-of-State			
Book Loans	2961	3705	25.13%
Photocopies	1324	1521	14.88%
Subtotal	4285	5226	21.96%
Unfilled	4416	4787	08.40%
Total Out-of-State	8701	10013	15.07%

It is important to emphasize that supervisors should gather statistics that will prove useful in analyzing departmental activities. Depending upon the individual situation, the ILL department may also be called upon to provide data on items requested by patrons for collection development use. Boucher (1997, 134-135) provides an excellent framework for organizing ILL statistics.

Statistics are also available externally from the major bibliographic utilities that you might use. OCLC provides its ILL Management Statistics on a monthly basis, while DOCLINE provides its users with statistics on a quarterly basis. Visit the website of the bibliographic utility or contact them for more information on available statistics.

QUALITATIVE ASSESSMENT

Littlejohn and Wales, in their 1996 article on assessment plans for ILL departments, provide a comprehensive plan for fully assessing an ILL department through three assessments: one for client satisfaction, one for internal peer review, and one for an "Operations Review"(7).

Based on an instrument developed at the University of Iowa, the operations review asks questions about bottlenecks in daily activities, activities that produce the most aggravation, and about which activities should be retained in, or eliminated from, the workflow. The finished review is expected to concentrate on ". . . changes that will reduce stress. . . [, that] will improve collegiality and cooperation. . . [and that will help with the] elimination of obsolete procedures" (16).

Departments conducting an initial assessment may need to slightly modify the questions to suit their particular needs, and may also wish to add new questions regarding electronic requesting and delivery of ILL requests (if those services are available to patrons).

RESOURCES

Consult the Management section in *Part II: Resources* for a list of readings and websites to assist you in managing the ILL department.

WORKS CITED

Boucher, Virginia. 1997. Interlibrary Loan Practices Handbook. 2nd ed. Chicago: American Library Association.
Littlejohn, Nancy, and Barbara Wales. 1996. "Assessment Plan for Interlibrary Loan Departments at Academic Libraries." *Journal of Interlibrary Loan, Document Delivery & Information Supply*, 7(2): 3-18.

Chapter 7

Additional Considerations

SUMMARY. Chapter 7 discusses additional considerations an ILL department supervisor might face: handling requests from far-flung distance education students, providing a library photocopy service, or selecting a document supplier for unmediated ILL. The unique challenges of medical libraries are also discussed. *[Article copies available for a fee from The Haworth Document Delivery Service: 1-800-HAWORTH. E-mail address: <docdelivery@haworthpress.com> Website: <http://www.HaworthPress.com> © 2006 by The Haworth Press, Inc. All rights reserved.]*

KEYWORDS. Distance education, document supply, photocopy, medical libraries, DOCLINE®

DISTANCE EDUCATION

Many ILL departments today deal not only with local users, but also with far-flung students studying and attending courses via distance education. Serving distance education students can be a challenge for ILL departments.

Distance education [(DE)] is a method of teaching in which the students are not required to be physically present at a specific location during the term. Most often, regular mail is used to send writ-

[Haworth co-indexing entry note]: "Additional Considerations." Hilyer, Lee Andrew. Co-published simultaneously in *Journal of Interlibrary Loan, Document Delivery & Electronic Reserve* (The Haworth Information Press, an imprint of The Haworth Press, Inc.) Vol. 16, No. 1/2, 2006, pp. 75-80; and: *Interlibrary Loan and Document Delivery: Best Practices for Operating and Managing Interlibrary Loan Services in All Libraries* (Lee Andrew Hilyer) The Haworth Information Press, an imprint of The Haworth Press, Inc., 2006, pp. 75-80. Single or multiple copies of this article are available for a fee from The Haworth Document Delivery Service [1-800-HAWORTH, 9:00 a.m. - 5:00 p.m. (EST). E-mail address: docdelivery@haworthpress.com].

ten material, videos, audiotapes, and CD-ROMs to the student and to turn in the exercises; nowadays e-mail and the Web are used as well. Often students are required to come to meetings at regional offices on specific weekends, for example to take exams. Distance education is offered at all levels, but is most frequently an option for university-level studies. (From the Wikipedia <http://en.wikipedia.org/wiki/Distance_education>)

One of the challenges is the cost and staff time of shipping materials to remote patrons. Another growing issue is convincing lending libraries to send materials directly to another library's patron. More and more universities are beginning to offer some type of distance education, and ILL departments must prepare policies and procedures to best meet the needs of DE students.

DOCUMENT SUPPLIERS

The years 1994-1998 saw tremendous growth in the number of document suppliers providing documents to both libraries and end users. The British Library Document Supply Centre, CISTI (Canada), KR SourceOne, Infotrieve, Information Express, and many more were either begun or tremendously expanded during those years. As market forces consolidated the market, many smaller players fell off the radar as the larger ones kept on growing. Document suppliers continue to play a role in today's ILL department.

Deciding to use a document supplier is based on many factors: departmental budget, time period in which the information is needed, convenience, and others. Many document suppliers include the copyright fee as a part of the total cost of the document, saving staff time in the eliminated need to report copyright. It used to be that traditional ILL was extremely slow, and that document suppliers were seen as a way to improve service. With the technological changes in the ILL department, this is no longer exactly the case, but they remain an effective and efficient option for many types of requests.

LIBRARY PHOTOCOPY SERVICE

Many ILL departments also operate additional services that do not fit neatly into the category of "borrowing " or "lending." Photocopy services, services where the library provides copies of articles and/or book loans from its own collections to its own patrons. Photocopy services save time for busy physicians, researchers, and local businesses, and are often relied upon to generate revenue to offset other costs in the ILL department.

Creation and Organization

Libraries may already have an existing photocopy service, or they may wish to establish one to generate service revenue. It is relatively easy to start one, as many of the ILL request management systems include modules specifically for the tracking and processing of photocopy requests.

If an ILL request management system is not available, you can easily create a web-to-e-mail request form or simple database system (Access, MySQL) to track requests. For low-use situations, a simple paper form may suffice.

Fee Structure

Some photocopy services charge a base fee plus a per-page fee; others charge a flat per-request fee. You may establish different categories of fees based on the user's affiliation with your library. The HAM-TMC Library in Houston, for example, uses a two-tiered system with one set of fees for cardholders and a slightly-higher fee schedule for non-cardholders. Similarly, you may establish fee structures based on the type of user you are serving. For example, students, faculty, and staff may pay lower fees than local businesses that use your service.

You may charge additional fees for expedited service, certain methods of delivery, or other value-added services. To help defray the costs of staff keying in received requests, as well as to encourage users to submit requests via the Web, the HAM-TMC Library charges a $1.00 per citation fee for requests submitted via fax or e-mail. Rice University Library's former document delivery service, R.i.C.E., charged approximately $10.00 extra for RUSH service.

Medical libraries must be careful to examine their responsibilities with respect to the national permitted maximum amount that can be charged. This is especially true for Loansome Doc requests (see later).

Daily Operation

Law firms and local businesses are often in need of information during the course of their business day. Rice University Library's former service, R.i.C.E., served a large number of clients in the oil and gas industry, owing to the specialized nature of the Library's collection. Operated on a cost-recovery basis, as are the services offered at HAM-TMC Library, revenues generated were used to support a variety of existing library programs.

Medical libraries, often through Loansome Doc, can meet the needs of physicians in private practice, biotechnology companies, local healthcare and social service organizations, and law firms.

Managing a photocopy services component is unique in that it contains elements of both borrowing and lending–as in lending, you must retrieve and copy material for the user, while you handle requests from your own patrons just as you do in your borrowing operation. Many libraries now utilize a web interface for their photocopy service, which allows patrons to submit requests, view request history, and monitor the status of their requests.

The HAM-TMC Library operates a vigorous photocopy service and the alignment of duties in the department allows for maximum efficiency. The Photocopy Services coordinator prints received requests from ILLiad, then passes them to the Library Assistant, who incorporates those photocopy requests with the day's waiting lending requests and retrieves the materials from the stacks.

Once journal volumes and books are retrieved from the stacks, articles and chapters are usually scanned and converted to Acrobat PDF files and posted to the user's ILLiad account for retrieval. Other delivery options include postal mail, fax, or pickup at the library's Circulation desk. Libraries considering establishing a photocopy service should plan for a wide variety of delivery methods to accommodate as many users as possible.

The beauty of an ILL request management system such as Clio or ILLiad is that it helps ILL staff to automate many of the previously tedious and time-consuming chores involved with processing requests. Elimination of these repetitive activities frees staff up to better manage their workflow, helping to reduce turnaround time and ensure smooth operation. It also permits staff to spend more time on difficult verifications or special projects, such as a suite of documents that need to be shipped at one time, or to a different address than the original requestor.

As with borrowing and lending requests, ILL departments must be aware and in compliance with applicable copyright laws with respect to photocopy services.

Invoicing can be accomplished manually, in conjunction with the library's Accounting department, or directly in a billing-capable ILL request management system.

MEDICAL LIBRARIES

Introduction

Medical libraries handle their ILL in a different manner than regular academic or public libraries. The vast majority of ILL traffic among medical libraries consists of journal articles, as in medicine there is an ongoing need for the latest and best information, usually found only in journal articles.

Organization

Medical libraries in the United States are organized into a hierarchical system known as the National Network of Libraries of Medicine (NN/LM). With the National Library of Medicine at the top, the network is divided into eight U.S. regions, with additional sections for Canada and Mexico.

Each region has a Regional Medical Library, or RML. The RML serves as the "lender of last resort" in a particular region, with Resource (RL) and Primary Access (PAL) libraries residing further down the network. PALs include the numerous hospital and clinic libraries which serve as the primary medical information access point for the nurses and physicians in those facilities.

DOCLINE®

Medical libraries generally rely on the web-based DOCLINE® system developed by the National Library of Medicine for the bulk of their requesting needs, though they may also utilize OCLC and RLIN for other material requests. DOCLINE was launched in March of 1985 and currently serves over 3,500 libraries in the U.S. and Canada.

Use of DOCLINE is free of charge to participating NN/LM members, though participation requires that libraries join the network and enter and maintain updated serial holdings. Unlike OCLC, which contains records at the source level, DOCLINE was designed to fully integrate with the MEDLINE (PubMed) database which contains article-level citations. DOCLINE users can submit requests for monographs and audiovisual materials, but most libraries utilize OCLC for these types of requests and limit their DOCLINE borrowing to journal articles. Libraries often verify NLM's monograph holdings through LOCATORplus, NLM's OPAC, which is accessible from within DOCLINE.

Unlike OCLC, the NN/LM imposes a maximum allowable charge for ILL transactions among network members. Currently, the network maximum for loans to libraries within a region is $9.00, while loans to members outside of your region can be no more than $11.00. DOCLINE members must also meet shorter response and turnaround time requirements than OCLC users because of the often urgent need for medical information by physicians and nurses. Like OCLC, DOCLINE automatically reroutes requests to the next lender if a library fails to respond to a request, or to update the request within the allotted time period.

Loansome Doc, an unmediated document requesting system, resides as a module within DOCLINE. DOCLINE libraries can elect to participate in the Loansome Doc service, which permits their authorized users to search the PubMed database and send requests for articles directly to their library's DOCLINE system, either for fulfillment from the library's own collection, or by another library through the available referral option.

The DOCUSER module within DOCLINE is an online database of DOCLINE library information and ILL policies. Libraries use the DOCUSER module to modify and extend their routing tables, which are similar to OCLC's Custom Holdings. Libraries set up lists of libraries in a series of cells, which DOCLINE then uses to match serial holdings information from SERHOLD. DOCLINE then routes the request to the library that owns the material.

RESOURCES

For more information on all of the above topics, consult *Part II: Resources.*

PART II:
RESOURCES

SUMMARY. The Resources section is an annotated list of books, articles, websites, and more that can be consulted during the ILL process. Materials included in the Resources section can assist with problem request verification, identification of potential suppliers, handling rare or fragile materials, automating the ILL process, and much more. Also included are some titles of historical interest, for those looking to understand the earlier practices and history of interlibrary loan. *[Article copies available for a fee from The Haworth Document Delivery Service: 1-800-HAWORTH. E-mail address: <docdelivery@haworthpress.com> Website: <http://www.HaworthPress.com> © 2006 by The Haworth Press, Inc. All rights reserved.]*

KEYWORDS. Background, copyright, ILL management systems, resources

BACKGROUND

DDILL (Document Delivery and Interlibrary Loan) Services Guide
Harwell, Jonathan, and Julie Harwell.
http://www.ddill.org

Like "Focus on Interlibrary Loan" (see later), this site strives to be a comprehensive online resource for Interlibrary Loan and Resource

---

[Haworth co-indexing entry note]: "Resources." Hilyer, Lee Andrew. Co-published simultaneously in *Journal of Interlibrary Loan, Document Delivery & Electronic Reserve* (The Haworth Information Press, an imprint of The Haworth Press, Inc.) Vol. 16, No. 1/2, 2006, pp. 81-106; and: *Interlibrary Loan and Document Delivery: Best Practices for Operating and Managing Interlibrary Loan Services in All Libraries* (Lee Andrew Hilyer) The Haworth Information Press, an imprint of The Haworth Press, Inc., 2006, pp. 81-106. Single or multiple copies of this article are available for a fee from The Haworth Document Delivery Service [1-800-HAWORTH, 9:00 a.m. - 5:00 p.m. (EST). E-mail address: docdelivery@haworthpress.com].

Sharing issues. Unfortunately, it too, is out-of-date. As of this writing, the site was last updated on December 9, 2003. Consider it a secondary resource, though many of the links are still active.

Developing Library and Information Center Collections
Evans, G. Edward. Englewood, CO: Libraries Unlimited. 1995.

This is a basic textbook on collection development. Evans discusses ILL several times throughout the text.

Focus on Interlibrary Loan
Chicago Library System.
http://www.chilibsys.org/CE/ILL/Default.htm

Focus on Interlibrary Loan is a website devoted to ILL issues, including links to policy documents, an ILL primer, and additional resources. Readers should note that there is no listed date on the web pages, and it appears that the site has not been updated in several years. Some of the information continues to be relevant today, so it may be worth Bookmarking for occasional reference.

How to Get What You Don't Have: A Guide to Obtaining Loans, Photocopies or Microcopies of Sci-Tech Publications
Piternick, Anne. Ottawa, ON: National Research Council Canada. 1973.

For anyone interested in a historical view of Interlibrary Loan, it is beneficial to review some of the texts written before the advent of bibliographic utilities and other systems that make ILL so much more accessible.

This practical guide still has much to offer to today's ILL department. Appendix J: Transliteration of Russian, for example, is extremely useful for puzzling out citations written in Cyrillic, while Appendix K: Abbreviations of Words Denoting Periodicals . . . provides a quick-reference guide to foreign-language terms denoting periodicals such as *Abhandlungen*, *Raboti*, *Sitzungsberichte*, and many more.

ILLWEB
Hollerich, Mary. 2001.
http://www.law.northwestern.edu/lawlibrary/illweb/

Like "Focus on Interlibrary Loan" and "DDILL," ILLWEB attempts to provide a one-stop resource for ILL tools, policies, and services. Unfortunately, also like the other two, the site has not been maintained.

Interlibrary Loan and Document Delivery

Arnold, Gretchen Naisawald and Martha R. Fishel. In: *Information Access and Delivery in Health Sciences Libraries.* Carolyn E. Lipscomb, Editor. Lanham, MD: Medical Library Association and The Scarecrow Press, Inc. 1996.

This chapter provides basic information on ILL in a medical library. Of special interest is the detailed explanation of the National Network of Libraries of Medicine (NN/LM). The volume is part of a series entitled Current Practice in Health Sciences Librarianship.

Interlibrary Loan and Document Delivery in the Larger Academic Library: A Guide for University, Research and Larger Public Libraries

Hilyer, Lee Andrew. Binghamton, NY: The Haworth Press, Inc., 2002. http://www.haworthpress.com

Containing valuable information on the day-to-day operation of an ILL department, it serves as a practical handbook and companion volume to this one. While many things have changed in the ILL department since its original publication, much of the information remains useful to ILL departments today.

In particular, see Chapter 6 for more in-depth information on crafting an effective patron borrowing policy.

Interlibrary Loan Practices HandBook, 2nd Edition

Boucher, Virginia. Chicago: American Library Association. 1997.

Whether you work in a medical library, academic library, law or public library, no ILL department should be without a copy of Boucher's handbook. By dint of the amount of change that ILL has undergone since publication of the second edition in 1997, it is in need of revision and updating to include more of the electronic resources that ILL departments have come to rely upon. It is comprehensive in scope with respect to paper verification sources, and its wealth of resources are certain to be useful when tracking down more difficult requests.

Interlibrary Loan/Document Delivery and Customer Satisfaction: Strategies for Redesigning Services

Pat L. Weaver-Myers, Editor. Binghamton, NY: The Haworth Press, Inc. 1996.

A compilation of articles focused on customer satisfaction with ILL services, this book is a useful starting point for anyone interested in evaluating and improving their ILL customer service.

Interlibrary Loan: Theory and Management
Gilmer, Lois C. Englewood, CO: Libraries Unlimited. 1994.

In ten years, the ILL landscape has changed dramatically from that which Gilmer describes in this 1994 volume, one of the few full-length monographic treatments of ILL. Of special note is the intriguing historical overview found in Chapter 1.

Locating Books for Interlibrary Loan: With a Bibliography of Printed Aids Which Show Location of Books in American Libraries
Winchell, Constance M. New York: H. W. Wilson. 1930.

When you have 100 rush requests to process, your student workers all called in sick, and your Internet connection is down, you may wish for simpler times in your department. Browsing through this early volume on ILL will provide you with much-needed perspective.

Part I is a lively and detailed history of ILL activity from approximately 1876 to 1930. Part II is a bibliography of printed library and union catalogs available during the 1920s and 1930s. ILL librarians dealing with requests for older materials might even find some of the listings still useful (provided the finding aids are still available).

National Network of Libraries of Medicine (NN/LM)
http://nnlm.gov

The United States medical library community is organized into a hierarchical network known as the National Network of Libraries of Medicine. See Chapter 9 for more information on special considerations for ILL in medical libraries.

Resource Sharing
Smith, Malcolm. *World Encyclopedia of Library and Information Services*. R. Wedgeworth, Editor. Chicago: American Library Association. 1993.

A fun read for devoted ILL librarians, it provides an enjoyable history of resource sharing in libraries.

BORROWING–VERIFICATION

American Library Directory
American Library Association. New Providence, NJ: R. R. Bowker. 2004.

http://www.ala.org

Arranged by state, this directory provides contact and address information, as well as descriptive data about individual libraries.

Catalog of U.S. Government Publications
U.S. Government Printing Office. Washington, DC: US GPO. 2004.

http://www.gpoaccess.gov/cgp/index.html

http://www.gpoaccess.gov/index.html (Main page for GPO)

In print and online, this is your first stop when researching government publications, especially those published by departments of the Executive branch (Department of Energy, Environmental Protection Agency, Department of Health and Human Services, etc.).

CISTI (Canada Institute for Science and Technology)
National Resources Council-Canada.

http://cisti-icist.nrc-cnrc.gc.ca/cisti_e.shtml

http://www.nrc-cnrc.gc.ca/main_e.html

One of the finest document delivery services in the world, CISTI consistently provides a high level of service coupled with easy-to-use services and amazing turnaround time from its extensive STM journal collection.

Collections Canada
National Library of Canada.

http://www.collectionscanada.ca/index-e.html

The online catalog for the National Library of Canada, who does provide ILL service through OCLC (as a lender of last resort).

Chemical Abstracts Service Source Index: 1907-1999 Cumulative (CASSI)

Chemical Abstracts Service. Columbus, OH: Chemical Abstracts Service. 2000.

http://www.cas.org/PRINTED/cassi.html

http://www.cas.org

CASSI is a useful tool for deciphering difficult STM journal title abbreviations. Naturally, it covers a large amount of chemistry-related titles, but is also useful for journal titles in medicine and physics.

Google (search engine)

Google, Inc.

http://www.google.com

Google has risen to be the number one search engine, as evidenced by the evolution of the word "google" and its use as a verb, as in: "Let's google it and see what we find." It is extremely useful for verifying problematic citations. Google's default operator is AND, so it does not need to be included in your search string, however, OR and NOT should be spelled out.

One of the newest developments with potential direct impact on libraries is the Open WorldCat pilot project. Google has harvested approximately 500,000 records of a total two million sent from OCLC. By restricting their search to a specific site (site: <worldcatlibraries.org>), users can retrieve WorldCat records in their Google searches. Denoted by the phrase "Find in a Library," clicking on one of these records yields a brief record display with a form for the user to enter their ZIP code. OCLC then limits the holdings display to local libraries based on the user's ZIP code.

Rather than try to directly compete with Google, OCLC continues to leverage the value of the WorldCat database and sustains its mission of supporting libraries and library services, no matter where the user might be.

ILL Policies Directory

OCLC.

http://illpolicies.oclc.org

The successor to OCLC's Name-Address Directory (NAD), this web-based service also provides an online alternative to the printed OCLC Participating Institutions guides.

Interlibrary Loan Policies Directory, 7th Edition
Morris, Leslie. New York: Neal-Schuman. 2002.
http://www.lesmorris.com/ILLPD%20Page.htm

Morris' directory provides an at-a-glance resource for library ILL policies–especially useful when handling requests for rare or difficult materials, or for when you wish to establish reciprocal agreements with other libraries.

Library of Congress
Library of Congress. Washington, DC: Library of Congress.
http://www.loc.gov

You can access the online catalog and other resources of the Library of Congress at the URL listed above.

List of Journals Indexed in Index Medicus
National Library of Medicine. Bethesda, MD: National Library of Medicine. 2003.
http://www.ncbi.nlm.nih.gov/entrez/query.fcgi?db=journals

An excellent source for deciphering medical journal titles; indispensable within a medical library. Also available online through PubMed.

LocatorPLUS
National Library of Medicine. Bethesda, MD: National Library of Medicine.
http://locatorplus.gov/

This is the National Library of Medicine's online catalog, which is also available from within the DOCLINE interface and the end-user NLM Gateway.

The British Library
British Library. London, UK.
http://www.bl.uk/catalogues/listings.html
http://blpc.bl.uk/

Web-based OPAC of the British Library. In addition to the British Library Public Catalogue, there are numerous additional catalogs to search, including ones for manuscripts, maps, newspapers, current serials, and more.

Ulrich's Standard Periodical Directory
New Providence, NJ: R. R. Bowker. 2003.
http://www.ulrichsweb.com/ulrichsweb/

Ulrich's is especially useful for locating ISSNs (International Standard Serial Numbers). Entries also include indexing locations (helpful for re-verifying citations) and document supplier availability (for those patrons who want RUSH service).

U.S. Patent and Trademark Office
U.S. Patent and Trademark Office. Washington, DC: USPTO.
http://www.uspto.gov

From the USPTO website:

"For over 200 years, the basic role of the United States Patent and Trademark Office (USPTO) has remained the same: to promote the progress of science and the useful arts by securing for limited times to inventors the exclusive right to their respective discoveries (Article 1, Section 8 of the United States Constitution). Under this system of protection, American industry has flourished. New products have been invented, new uses for old ones discovered, and employment opportunities created for millions of Americans. The strength and vitality of the U.S. economy depends directly on effective mechanisms that protect new ideas and investments in innovation and creativity. The continued demand for patents and trademarks underscores the ingenuity of American inventors and entrepreneurs. The USPTO is at the cutting edge of the Nation's technological progress and achievement.

"The USPTO is a federal agency in the Department of Commerce. The agency is consolidating its facilities from 18 buildings spread throughout Crystal City in Arlington, Virginia, to five interconnected buildings in Alexandria, Virginia. The USPTO began occupying the first two buildings in December 2003, and full occupancy is scheduled by mid-2005. The office employs over 6,500 full-time staff to support its major functions–the examination and issuance of patents and the examination and registration of trademarks.

"The USPTO has evolved into a unique government agency. Since 1991–under the Omnibus Budget Reconciliation Act (OBRA) of 1990–the agency has been fully fee funded. The primary services the agency provides include processing patent and trademark applications and disseminating patent and trademark information" (http://www.uspto.gov/web/menu/intro.html).

LAWS AND REGULATIONS

Health Insurance Portability and Accountability Act of 1996 (HIPAA)
Public Law 104-191.
http://www.hhs.gov/news/facts/privacy.html
http://www.cms.hhs.gov/hipaa/default.asp?

HIPAA provides safeguards for the privacy and confidentiality of patient records. Medical libraries in particular must comply with HIPAA rules and even libraries not directly involved in patient care may be subject to HIPAA provisions. The HAM-TMC Library, for example, is an independent library serving the Texas Medical Center. While the Library is not housed within a hospital or other care facility, it nonetheless must comply with HIPAA rules because of computer network resources which are shared with a facility providing care.

USA PATRIOT Act
American Library Association. Chicago: American Library Association. 2004.
http://www.ala.org/ala/oif/ifissues/usapatriotact.htm

This site from the American Library Association provides additional information on the USA PATRIOT Act and how it affects libraries. ALA provides a link to a document entitled "What to Do If Served with a Search Warrant under USA PATRIOT Act" which gives additional instructions to libraries about dealing with search warrants and law enforcement personnel.

The Medical Library Association also provides information on the USA PATRIOT Act and other regulations in its "Governmental Relations" section of its website (https://www.mlanet.org/government/index.html).

USA PATRIOT Act
Public Law 107-056. 2002. 115 Stat. 272.

Short for "UNITING AND STRENGTHENING AMERICA BY PROVIDING APPROPRIATE TOOLS REQUIRED TO INTERCEPT AND OBSTRUCT TERRORISM," the USA PATRIOT Act supersedes any state laws governing confidentiality of library records and allows law enforcement officials to review and/or seize library records in the investigation of possible terrorist acts.

LAWS AND REGULATIONS–COPYRIGHT

Final Report (CONTU Guidelines on Photocopying under Interlibrary Loan Arrangements)

National Commission on New Technological Uses of Copyrighted Works (CONTU). Washington, DC: Library of Congress. 1979.
http://www.cni.org/docs/infopols/CONTU.html

All ILL department staff should be familiar with the basics of the CONTU Guidelines as well as the relevant sections of title 17 U.S.C. The CONTU Guidelines document can be found at the website listed above. Additionally, CNI provides access to a number of information policy documents, such as model ILL codes and policy documents on copyright and other issues. See http://www.cni.org/docs/infopols for a full listing. ·

Constitution of the United States of America

United States of America. 1787.

Article I, Section 8, Clause 8: The Congress shall have Power "To promote the Progress of Science and useful Arts, by securing for limited Times to Authors and Inventors the exclusive Right to their respective Writings and Discoveries"; this is the Constitutional clause providing for copyright and patent protections.

Copyright and Intellectual Property

Association of Research Libraries. Washington, DC.
http://www.arl.org/info/frn/copy/copytoc.html

ARL's copyright web pages are well-organized and well-divided into categories such as "Recent Statutes," "Court Cases/Legal Decisions," and "Resources." The site is being kept current (last updated July 20, 2005) and should be added to your Bookmark file for copyright resources.

Copyright Basics

U.S. Copyright Office. Washington, DC: U.S. Copyright Office. 2000. Circular 1.
http://www.copyright.gov/circs/circ1.html

Copyright Basics is the first in a series of circulars providing information on copyright for both inventors and researchers. PDF and

HTML versions are available, and the text has now also been translated into Spanish.

Copyright Clearance Center
http://www.copyright.com

The CCC's website offers online permissions and royalty payments. CCC is the RRO for the United States–most libraries pay online. CCC recently moved to a flat per-transaction fee schedule. New partnerships and connections with other library services are making it easier for libraries to pay copyright royalties and to remain in compliance with copyright law.

Copyright Considerations for Fee-Based Document Delivery Services
Gasaway, Laura N. *Journal of Interlibrary Loan, Document Delivery & Information Supply*. 1999. 10 (1): 75-92.

Still an excellent article on the often-complicated issue of copyright with respect to fee-based or cost-recovery library services.

Copyright Management Center, IUPUI
Copyright Management Center. Indianapolis, IN.
http://www.copyright.iupui.edu/

Though this online copyright resource is intended for IUPUI and the larger Indiana University community, its resources are of benefit to any ILL department. The CMC's director, Kenneth Crews, writes extensively on copyright and fair use, and his explanations of the law and his guidance are extremely clear and easy-to-understand.

Copyright of Electronic Materials
Morgan Davis, Linda. *Technology Fact Sheets*. National Network of Libraries of Medicine–South Central Region. 2003.
http://nnlm.gov/scr/techsheets/lmorgan.html

A concise "fact-sheet" on the uses of copyrighted electronic materials, this document provides you with a quick three-point rule-of-thumb, as well as information on related topics. It includes plenty of web links to additional resources and articles.

Copyright Office, United States

U.S. Copyright Office. Washington, DC: U.S. Copyright Office. http://www.copyright.gov

The website for the U.S. Copyright Office provides information to authors pursuing copyright for their intellectual works, as well as advice and instruction on the use of copyrighted materials.

Checklist for Fair Use. Appendix E

Crews, Kenneth D. In: *Copyright Essentials for Librarians and Educators.* Chicago: American Library Association. 2000.

Appendix E is a checklist for determining whether or not use of copyrighted material meets the "fair use" standard. Use it as a guide when handling a difficult or unclear copyright situation.

Digital Millennium Copyright Act of 1998 (DMCA)

Public Law 105-304. 1998. 112 Stat. 2860, 2887.

The DMCA was enacted to amend title 17 of the U.S. Code (copyright) and to change U.S. law for full implementation of WIPO (World Intellectual Property Organization) treaties to which the U.S. is a signatory.

Filling from Full Text Databases: Interlibrary Loan Practice and Licensing Language

Thompson-Young, Alexia. *Presented at the Fifth TexShare Interlibrary Loan Workshop, Dallas, TX, November 22, 2002.* http://www.texshare.edu/programs/ill/illworking/workshops/ workshop2002/workshop2002.html

Part of the program of the TexShare ILL workshop, this presentation [handout available online] provides some guidance on the filling of ILL requests using licensed electronic databases and journals.

Legal Solutions in Electronic Reserves and the Electronic Delivery of Interlibrary Loan

Croft, Janet Brennan. Binghamton, NY: The Haworth Press, Inc. 2004. http://www.haworthpress.com/web/JILIS

ILL librarians have been waiting for a book like this for a long time. Many books on copyright in libraries attempt to deal with all aspects of copyright as it relates to library service, thus limiting the information for ILL to a chapter or two at most.

Croft rectifies that situation with a thoroughly researched and easy-to-read handbook for dealing with the legal aspects of ILL service (also published as v. 14, n. 3 of the *Journal of Interlibrary Loan, Document Delivery & Information Supply*).

Memorandum August 19, 1999
Lutzker, Arnold P. 1999.
http://www.arl.org/info/frn/copy/notice.html

After the DMCA, questions arose regarding a library's requirement with respect to notices of copyright included with copies provided through Interlibrary Loan. This memorandum addresses the question of using a copyright "stamp" if no notice of copyright can be located on the item.

Selected Provisions from the U.S. Copyright Act. Appendix A
In: *Copyright Essentials for Librarians and Educators*. Crews, Kenneth, Editor. Chicago: American Library Association. 2000.

The sections of title 17 most relevant to everyday ILL operation are found in this Appendix to Crews' excellent monograph on copyright.

Sonny Bono Copyright Term Extension Act
Public Law 105-298. 1998. 112 Stat. 2827.

PL 105-298 also amends portion of title 17 of the U.S. Code, especially with respect to the length of term of copyright protection. Visit Georgia Harper's UT Crash Course in Copyright for more information on this law.

The UT System Crash Course in Copyright
Harper, Georgia. Austin, TX: University of Texas General Counsel's Office. 2001.
http://www.utsystem.edu/ogc/IntellectualProperty/cprtindx.htm#top

If you haven't already encountered or heard a recommendation about this website, you've been living under a rock. Harper's "crash course" is one of the most useful and comprehensive sites on copyright for the academic community.

UCLA Library Copyright Policy

University of California-Los Angeles (UCLA). Los Angeles, CA: UCLA. 2003.

http://www.library.ucla.edu/copyright /index.html

An excellent example of a clear and easy-to-navigate comprehensive library copyright policy. All of UCLA's procedures and policies are spelled out for users and library staff alike. Reliance on text links instead of heavy graphics adds tremendously to the site's ease-of-use.

United States Code

United States of America. 1976. Title 17, sec. 107.

http://www.copyright.gov/title17/

Copyright law is codified in Title 17 of the United States Code.

When Works Pass into the Public Domain

Gasaway, Laura N. 1999.

http://www.unc.edu/~unclng/public-d.htm

Use this excellent and easy-to-understand chart when attempting to determine if a work is still covered by copyright law, or if it has passed into the public domain.

LENDING

International Lending and Document Delivery: Principles and Guidelines for Procedure

IFLA. 2001.

http://www.ifla.org/VI/2/p3/ildd.htm

ILL departments, no matter how small, are encouraged to lend internationally whenever possible. IFLA's Guidelines are useful for departments seeking to begin international lending.

EFTS–Electronic Funds Transfer System

University of Connecticut Health Center. Farmington, CT. 2004.

https://efts.uchc.edu

Similar in functionality to OCLC's IFM (Interlibrary Loan Fee Management) service, EFTS is an electronic-billing system used by medical libraries to facilitate debits and credits for ILL activity, mainly on the DOCLINE system. The National Library of Medicine is committed to expanding the program nationally to all National Network of Libraries of Medicine (NN/LM) members.

MANAGEMENT

Guidelines for the Preparation of Policies on Library Access
ACRL Access Policy Guidelines Task Force. 1992.
http://www.ala.org/ala/acrl/acrlstandards/guidelinespreparation.htm

ACRL provides clear and detailed instructions for preparing library access policies, including those for ILL.

Stop and Go-Managing ILL Traffic
Carriveau, Ken, and Jeff Steely. *Presented at the Fifth TexShare Interlibrary Loan Workshop, Dallas, TX, November 22, 2002.*
http://www.texshare.edu/programs/ill/illworking/workshops/
workshop2002/workshop2002.html

Presented at the TexShare (Texas) ILL workshop in November 2002, Carriveau and Steely's presentation documents the Baylor University Library ILL department's workflow streamlining and re-engineering that have enabled them to significantly reduce turnaround time and to eliminate unnecessary steps in the ILL process.

Upward Appraisal: What Do Subordinates Consider Important in Evaluating Their Supervisors?
Rubin, Richard. *Library & Information Science Research.* 1995. 17:
151-161.

Rubin's article played an important role in my development as a manager when I first arrived at the HAM-TMC Library, having supervised only student workers in previous positions. The article does not include the original instrument used for evaluation, but I was able to craft my own upward appraisal form for use in my ILL department. I crafted a set of 20 questions with responses to be returned using a Likert scale (1-5). For more information on upward appraisal, see Chapter 6.

MANAGEMENT–ASSESSMENT AND EVALUATION

Assessment Plan for Interlibrary Loan Departments at Academic Libraries

Littlejohn, Nancy, and Barbara Wales. *Journal of Interlibrary Loan, Document Delivery & Information Supply.* 1996. 7(2): 3-18.

Although this article is nearly ten-years-old, its themes of service evaluation, needs assessment, and customer service continue to remain important to ILL departments. Review the included appendices for an excellent starting point for a full-scale evaluation of your own department.

MANAGEMENT–COSTING

Appendix I: Cost Worksheets

Jackson, Mary. *Measuring the Performance of Interlibrary Loan Operations in North American Research and College Libraries.* Washington, DC: Association of Research Libraries. 1998.
http://www.arl.org

Jackson's worksheets for determining cost categories are clear and easy-to-use.

Assessing ILL/DD Services Study: Initial Observations

Jackson, Mary E. *ARL Bulletin.* Washington, DC: Association of Research Libraries. 2003. No. 230/231.

Brief communication about the latest Assessing ILL/DD Services study, which collected 2001-2002 performance and cost data in research, academic, and special libraries. Jackson's earlier study (1998) revealed insights about high-performing borrowing and lending operations, which led to a series of ARL workshops on the topic. Further analysis is being conducted on the data gathered in 2002.

Measuring the Performance of Interlibrary Loan Operations in North American Research and College Libraries

Jackson, Mary. Washington, DC: Association of Research Libraries. 1998.
http://www.arl.org

Presenting the results of the 1998 ARL ILL/DD Performance Measures Study, Jackson's findings identified the characteristics of high-performing borrowing and lending operations, characteristics which, when applied to a library's ILL operation, yielded improvements in productivity and efficiency in many departments across the country. Another study was undertaken in 2001-02, but because different libraries participated in different years, Jackson is undertaking additional statistical analysis on the 46 libraries who participated in both the 1998 and the 2001-02 studies. As of May 2004, no additional published results of the 01-02 study were available. Check in with the ARL website for news and announcements about the results.

Methodologies for Determining Costs of Interlibrary Lending and Interlibrary Borrowing

Dickson, Stephen P., and Virginia Boucher. *Research Access Through New Technology.* Mary E. Jackson, Editor. New York: AMS Press. 1989. 137-159.

If you are considering conducting a cost analysis of your ILL service, start here with Dickson and Boucher's article. Supplement your reading of this article with Mary Jackson's 1998 ARL study.

PROFESSIONAL DEVELOPMENT–ASSOCIATIONS

American Library Association

http://www.ala.org

The librarian's primary professional association, ALA provides guidance on ILL and document delivery issues, as well as advocating for the profession as a whole.

IFLANET

International Federation of Library Associations.
http://www.ifla.org

The website of the International Federation of Library Associations and Institutions provides information and news on developments and trends in the international library community.

MLANET

Medical Library Association.
http://www.mlanet.org

MLANET is the website for the Medical Library Association (MLA), the medical librarian's primary professional association. The site provides in-depth information on a wide range of topics relevant to today's medical library.

Special Libraries Association
Special Libraries Association.
http://www.sla.org

Like the Medical Library Association, the Special Libraries Association (SLA) is a professional association for librarians who work (or have an interest) in special libraries such as corporate libraries, one-person libraries, law libraries, etc.

PROFESSIONAL DEVELOPMENT–DISCUSSION LISTS

ARIE-L
http://listserv.boisestate.edu/archives/arie-l.html

ARIE-L is the discussion list for ARIEL document transmission software users. ARIEL is ubiquitous in most libraries across the U.S., so you can find information, tips and tricks, and much more for and about ARIEL on this list. To subscribe, visit the website listed above.

ILLiad-L
From the welcome e-mail:
"ILLiad-L is an open, un-moderated discussion forum for users of ILLiad, the complete interlibrary loan/document delivery system. ILLiad-L is a service of the Virginia Tech Interlibrary Loan Department, where ILLiad was born on March 17, 1997, and the Virginia Tech listserv office."

Listserv for all things ILLiad–great for getting technical help with customization.

To join ILLiad-L, send a message to: LISTSERV@LISTSERV. VT.EDU: SUBSCRIBE ILLIAD-L YourFirstName YourLastName.

ILL-L
Hollerich, Mary (Moderator).

ILL-L is a lively and active discussion list centered on ILL. Moderated by Mary Hollerich, every ILL librarian should be subscribed to ILL-L, not only for its news and information, but also for its use as a method of requesting assistance with difficult citations or hard-to-find materials.

To subscribe, send the message "subscribe ILL-L firstname lastname" to LISTPROC@nwu.edu.

OCLC-SHARING-L (Broadcast-only)
https://www3.oclc.org/app/listserv/sharingl/

To help users stay abreast of information relating to the full integration of resource sharing services with the FirstSearch reference service, OCLC has established this broadcast-only e-mail discussion list for users. Periodic notices are sent regarding key migration milestones and sunset dates.

PROFESSIONAL DEVELOPMENT–
RECOMMENDED READING

Interlending and Document Supply
http://ariel.emeraldinsight.com/vl=1425214/cl=21/nw=1/rpsv/ilds.htm

IDS pursues a more international scope than the *Journal of Interlibrary Loan, Document Delivery & Electronic Reserve.* Its frequent articles reviewing recent ILL/DD literature are handy for keeping up with broad trends.

Interlibrary Loan Weblog
Hilyer, Lee Andrew.
http://illresources.blogspot.com/

Created in May 2004 and updated regularly, this log provides current news and information about ILL happenings. Author may occasionally post commentary on ILL issues to spark discussion within the community.

Journal of Interlibrary Loan, Document Delivery & Electronic Reserve
http://www.haworthpress.com/web/JILDD/
http://www.haworthpress.com
http://www.lesmorris.com/JILIS%20Page.htm

Renamed in 2005 to reflect a shift in focus, the *Journal* is THE "must-read" journal for U.S. Interlibrary Loan practitioners. Former name: *Journal of Interlibrary Loan, Document Delivery & Information Supply.*

Journal of Library & Information Services in Distance Learning
http://www.haworthpress.com

A new journal begun in 2004, it deals solely with issues relating to the provision of library services to distance education (DE) students. Since many ILL departments already handle DE requests, consider adding it to your list of regular professional reading.

NLM Technical Bulletin
Bethesda, MD: National Library of Medicine.
http://www.nlm.nih.gov/pubs/techbull/

NLM's Technical Bulletin is a must-read for medical libraries, since their operations and services are so closely tied with those of NLM. The Technical Bulletin provides up-to-date information on PubMed, DOCLINE, and other services provided by NLM.

OCLC ResearchWorks
http://www.oclc.org/research/researchworks

This is the website for OCLC's ResearchWorks, where they feature new technologies and cutting-edge information research.

TECHNOLOGY

Best Practice in Library/Information Technology Collaboration
Cowen, Janet L. and Jerry Edson. *Journal of Hospital Librarianship.* 2002. 2(4): 1-15.

Cowen and Edson's article provide some much-needed insight into the relationships between librarians and IT personnel. Barriers to communication and stereotypes that cause unneeded difficulties are discussed. This is an excellent article to help you build trust with your IT department whose help is required more and more within the ILL department.

Convergence of Interlibrary Loan and Local Collections
Huwe, Terence K. *Computers in Libraries.* March 2004. 34-36.

An interesting article discussing the convergence of ILL with local systems and services. Huwe discusses the California Digital Library's "'super' request form" which handles ILL transactions ". . . alongside of and in relationship to full-text sources"(35).

Huwe also emphasizes the continued importance of bibliographic elements in online records and how a basic understanding of those elements is essential to ILL and to retrieving the material the patron needs. He indicates that during the ILL requesting process is a valuable opportunity for teaching related skills such as formulating effective searches and finding articles within a multitude of databases.

Linkage between ILL and full-text resources reinforce each other and contribute to more effective identification and retrieval of relevant information sources.

TECHNOLOGY–BIBLIOGRAPHIC UTILITY

DOCLINE (Interlibrary Loan Request Routing and Referral System)
Bethesda, MD: National Library of Medicine. 2004.
http://docline.gov/docline/index.cfm

From the DOCLINE® FAQ:
"DOCLINE is the National Library of Medicine's automated interlibrary loan (ILL) request routing and referral system. The purpose of the system is to provide improved document delivery service among libraries in the National Network of Libraries of Medicine® (NN/LM) by linking journal holdings to efficiently route the requests to potential lending libraries on behalf of the borrower.

"Requests can be created, edited, routed, received, and filled in this system. DOCLINE participants can also check the status of requests for which they are either the borrowing or lending library.

"DOCLINE serves over 3,200 U.S., Canadian, and Mexican medical libraries at no cost. Some selected national and major medical libraries in other countries also have DOCLINE access. Health sciences libraries and libraries at institutions with a health sciences mission are eligible to apply for access to the DOCLINE system" (http://www.nlm.nih.gov/services/doc_what.html).

New Directions in Sharing
http://www.oclc.org/ill/migration/default.htm

As OCLC prepares to retire Passport for ILL, ILL Microenhancer, and the ILL Web interface, ILL functions are being folded into an enhanced FirstSearch interface, combining resource discovery with immediate staff creation of requests. In addition to technical concerns, OCLC also hopes to reduce the development costs associated with maintaining multiple interfaces, and to provide libraries with an enhanced and more efficient ILL interface.

OCLC Interlibrary Loan User Guide, 2nd Edition
OCLC. Dublin, OH: OCLC. 2000.
http://www.oclc.org/support/documentation/ill/using/userguide/

This guide describes in detail the features and operation of OCLC's ILL service. Libraries may still order print copies of the Guide, or access it directly on the Web. Due to the impending retirement of OCLC Passport software, another edition of the Guide will likely be issued in 2005.

Online Computer Library Center (OCLC)
http://www.oclc.org

From OCLC's website:
"Founded in 1967, OCLC Online Computer Library Center is a non-profit, membership, computer library service and research organization dedicated to the public purposes of furthering access to the world's information and reducing information costs. More than 50,000 libraries in 84 countries and territories around the world use OCLC services to locate, acquire, catalog, lend, and preserve library materials.

"Researchers, students, faculty, scholars, professional librarians, and other information seekers use OCLC services to obtain bibliographic, abstract, and full-text information when and where they need it.

"OCLC and its member libraries cooperatively produce and maintain WorldCat–the OCLC Online Union Catalog" (http://www.oclc.org/about/default.htm).

Research Libraries Group
http://www.rlg.org

The Research Libraries Group provides RLIN, a bibliographic database similar to OCLC's WorldCat, and resource sharing products such as its ISO-compliant ILL request management system, ILL Manager. RLG was also the original developer of the ARIEL document transmission software.

TECHNOLOGY–DATABASES

NLM Gateway
National Library of Medicine. Bethesda, MD.
http://gateway.nlm.nih.gov

To search multiple NLM resources at once, try using the NLM Gateway. Through a single search box, users can execute queries on MEDLINE/PubMed, LocatorPlus (NLM's catalog), MedlinePlus (consumer health), and others all at once.

PubMed
National Library of Medicine. Bethesda, MD.
http://www.ncbi.nlm.nih.gov/entrez/query.fcgi
http://www.ncbi.nlm.nih.gov/Entrez/index.html

PubMed, also known as the MEDLINE database, is THE source for article citations to the medical literature. It works seamlessly with NLM's DOCLINE system to facilitate document delivery transactions among medical libraries. PubMed Central is the database's full-text repository of electronic journals.

The tutorial (accessible from the left navigation bar) is extensive and provides an in-depth introduction to using and understanding PubMed. The MEDLINE database is also available in other formats from other vendors (OVID, CSA, etc.).

TECHNOLOGY–
INTERLIBRARY LOAN (ILL) MANAGEMENT SYSTEMS

Clio (ClioAdvanced)
http://www.cliosoftware.com

Clio (and ClioAdvanced), along with OCLC ILLiad, comprise the two most widely used ILL management systems. The standard version (Clio) provides staff with an efficient and extremely cost-effective solution to managing ILL transactions. ClioAdvanced includes a full-featured patron interface. Like OCLC ILLiad, ClioAdvanced is a complete ILL solution for your department.

Interlibrary Loan and Resource Sharing Products: An Overview of Current Features and Functionality

Jackson, Mary. *Library Technology Reports.* 2000. 36(6): 5-225.

This article is a compilation of responses to a questionnaire sent out by the author to vendors of ILL products. Because there is not an online equivalent, this is still currently the most comprehensive source of information on ILL request management systems (ILLiad, ILL Manager, Clio, etc.). Supplement your consultation of the printed issue with visits to vendor websites for the most up-to-date information.

OCLC ILLiad

Atlas Systems, Inc.; OCLC.

http://www.oclc.org/illiad/

http://www.atlas-sys.com

Originally launched at Virginia Tech in 1997, ILLiad was licensed by OCLC, Inc. and is now one of the leading ILL management systems in use today. ILLiad is ISO-compliant and features tight integration with OCLC.

TECHNOLOGY–SOFTWARE

ARIEL Document Transmission Software

Infotrieve. Los Angeles, CA.

http://www4.infotrieve.com/products_services/ariel.asp

Created originally by the Research Libraries Group, ARIEL software is used for the point-to-point ftp transmission of scanned articles in multi-page TIFF format. Now owned by Infotrieve, ARIEL also provides an "out-of-the-box" patron electronic delivery solution, as well as support for color scanning.

Prospero : An Open Source Internet Document Delivery (IDD) System

Prior Health Sciences Library, The Ohio State University. Columbus, OH.

http://bones.med.ohio-state.edu/prospero/

Prospero is a free, open-source patron document delivery system that offers users the ability to send documents to patrons either as e-mail attachments or to post them to a secure web server for patrons to download at their convenience.

TECHNOLOGY–STANDARDS

Building an OpenURL Resolver in Your Own Shop
Dahl, Mark. *Computers in Libraries*. 2004. 24(2): 6-8; 53-56.

Dahl's article is a practical, how-to article for technologically savvy librarians who wish to build their own OpenURL link resolver.

OpenURL, "[f]or most practical purposes . . . lets you create URLs that transmit bibliographic information" (Banerjee, 2004, 12). OpenURL is a framework for sending bibliographic information to a web page for processing, usually to retrieve the full text of a selected citation, or to pass the elements of a bibliographic citation to a service or system such as ILLiad for ILL request processing. "Standards like OpenURL make it possible for venders to link citations in Web pages to full text or request forms, or to create other products that can take advantage of clickable links containing bibliographic information"(14).

OpenURL can be implemented across a wide variety of systems and vendors: it is available in ILLiad, for example, to import citations from OCLC's FirstSearch databases such as ArticleFirst and Electronic Collections Online (ECO). It further helps to integrate disparate library services (OPAC, electronic journals, databases, ILL, etc.) into a more seamless experience for the user.

Interlibrary Loan Application Standards Maintenance Agency
http://www.lac-bac.gc.ca/iso/ill/main.htm

This website provides technical detail on the ISO ILL protocol, along with additional resources for understanding and implementing the protocol.

ISO ILL : The International Standard for Interlibrary Loan
http://www.oclc.org/isoill/default.htm

Here you will find concise and clear information on the ISO ILL protocol.

Know How to Integrate Services to Make Libraries Easier to Use
Banerjee, Kyle. *Computers in Libraries*. March 2004. 10-16.

This is a recent article discussing technologies now being implemented in libraries such as OpenURL and LDAP, and how to integrate those with existing standards such as MARC to better facilitate resource discovery. Technologies and their impact on the ILL department is discussed in the article.

The OpenURL and OpenURL Framework: Demystifying Link Resolution

Apps, Ann. *Ariadne.* 2004. (38): Unknown.
http://www.ariadne.ac.uk/issue38/apps-rpt/intro.html

A report of a one-day conference on OpenURL held in Washington, DC in 2003. Fairly technical in nature, it provides ample additional information on the projected future uses of OpenURL.

APPENDICES

Appendix A

National Interlibrary Loan Code

Interlibrary Loan Code for the United States

Prepared by the Interlibrary Loan Committee, Reference and User Services Association, 1994, revised 2001. Approved by the RUSA Board of Directors January 2001.

INTRODUCTION

The Reference and User Services Association, acting for the American Library Association in its adoption of this code recognizes that the sharing of material between libraries is an integral element in the provision of library service and believes it to be in the public interest to encourage such an exchange.

In the interest of providing quality service, libraries have an obligation to obtain material to meet the informational needs of users when local resources do not meet those needs. Interlibrary loan (ILL), a mechanism for obtaining material is essential to the vitality of all libraries.

Reprinted with permission from the American Library Association.

[Haworth co-indexing entry note]: "Appendix A. National Interlibrary Loan Code." Hilyer, Lee Andrew. Co-published simultaneously in *Journal of Interlibrary Loan, Document Delivery & Electronic Reserve* (The Haworth Information Press, an imprint of The Haworth Press, Inc.) Vol. 16, No. 1/2, 2006, pp. 107-110; and: *Interlibrary Loan and Document Delivery: Best Practices for Operating and Managing Interlibrary Loan Services in All Libraries* (Lee Andrew Hilyer) The Haworth Information Press, an imprint of The Haworth Press, Inc., 2006, pp. 107-110. Single or multiple copies of this article are available for a fee from The Haworth Document Delivery Service [1-800-HAWORTH, 9:00 a.m. - 5:00 p.m. (EST). E-mail address: docdelivery@haworthpress.com].

http://www.haworthpress.com/web/JILDD
© 2006 by The Haworth Press, Inc. All rights reserved.
doi:10.1300/J474v16n01_09

The effectiveness of the national interlibrary loan system depends upon participation of libraries of all types and sizes.

This code establishes principles that facilitate the requesting of material by a library and the provision of loans or copies in response to those requests. In this code, "material" includes books, audiovisual materials, and other returnable items as well as copies of journal articles, book chapters, excerpts, and other non-returnable items.

1.0 Definition

1.1 Interlibrary loan is the process by which a library requests material from, or supplies material to, another library.

2.0 Purpose

2.1 The purpose of interlibrary loan as defined by this code is to obtain, upon request of a library user, material not available in the user's local library.

3.0 Scope

3.1 This code is intended to regulate the exchange of material between libraries in the United States.

3.2 Interlibrary loan transactions with libraries outside of the United States are governed by the International Federation of Library Associations and Institutions' International Lending: Principles and Guidelines for Procedure.

4.0 Responsibilities of the Requesting Library

4.1 The requesting library should establish, maintain, and make available to its users an interlibrary borrowing policy.

4.2 It is the responsibility of the requesting library to ensure the confidentiality of the user.

4.3 Some requesting libraries permit users to initiate online interlibrary loan requests that are sent directly to potential supplying libraries. The requesting library assumes full responsibility for these user-initiated transactions.

4.4 Requested material should be described completely and accurately following accepted bibliographic practice.

4.5 The requesting library should identify libraries that own the requested material. The requesting library should check and adhere to the policies of potential supplying libraries.

4.6 When no libraries can be identified as owning the needed material, requests may be sent to libraries believed likely to own the material, accompanied by an indication that ownership is not confirmed.

4.7 The requesting library should transmit interlibrary loan requests electronically.

4.8 For copy requests, the requesting library must comply with the U.S. copyright law (Title 17, U.S. Code) and its accompanying guidelines.

4.9 The requesting library is responsible for borrowed material from the time it leaves the supplying library until it has been returned to and received by the supplying library. This includes all material shipped directly to and/or returned by the user. If damage or loss occurs, the requesting library is responsible for compensation or replacement, in accordance with the preference of the supplying library.

4.10 The requesting library is responsible for honoring the due date and enforcing any use restrictions specified by the supplying library. The due date is defined as the date the material is due to be checked-in at the supplying library.

4.11 The requesting library should normally request a renewal before the item is due. If the supplying library does not respond, the requesting library may assume that a renewal has been granted extending the due date by the same length of time as the original loan.

4.12 All borrowed material is subject to recall. The requesting library should respond immediately if the supplying library recalls an item.

4.13 The requesting library should package material to prevent damage in shipping and should comply with any special instructions stated by the supplying library.

4.14 The requesting library is responsible for following the provisions of this code. Disregard for any provision may be reason for suspension of service by a supplying library.

5.0 Responsibilities of the Supplying Library

5.1 The supplying library should establish, maintain, and make available an interlibrary lending policy.

5.2 The supplying library should consider filling all requests for material regardless of format, but has the right to determine what material will be supplied on a request by request basis.

5.3 It is the responsibility of the supplying library to ensure the confidentiality of the user.

5.4 The supplying library should process requests in a timely manner that recognizes the needs of the requesting library and/or the requirements of the electronic network or transmission system being used. If unable to fill a request, the supplying library should respond promptly and should state the reason the request cannot be filled.

5.5 When filling requests, the supplying library should send sufficient information with each item to identify the request.

5.6 The supplying library should indicate the due date and any restrictions on the use of the material and any special return packaging or shipping requirements. The due date is defined as the date the material is due to be checked-in at the supplying library.

5.7 The supplying library should ship material in a timely and efficient manner to the location specified by the requesting library. Loaned material should be packaged to prevent loss or damage in shipping. Copies should be delivered by electronic means whenever possible.

5.8 The supplying library should respond promptly to requests for renewals. If the supplying library does not respond, the requesting library may assume that a renewal has been granted extending the due date by the same length of time as the original loan.

5.9 The supplying library may recall material at any time.

5.10 The supplying library may suspend service to a requesting library that fails to comply with the provisions of this code.

Appendix B

Supplementary Material
to the National Interlibrary Loan Code

Interlibrary Loan Code for the United States

Explanatory Supplement for Use with the Interlibrary Loan Code for the United States (January 2001)

These Guidelines are intended to amplify specific sections of the Interlibrary Loan Code for the United States, providing fuller explanation and specific examples for text that is intentionally general and prescriptive. Topical headings in these Guidelines refer to the equivalent sections in the Code. Libraries are expected to comply with the Code, using the Guidelines as a source for general direction.[1]

Introduction

The U.S. Interlibrary Loan Code, first published in 1917 and adopted by The American Library Association in 1919, is designed to provide a code of behavior for requesting and supplying material within the United States. This code does not override consortial agreements and regional or state codes which may be more liberal or more prescriptive. This national code is intended to provide guidelines for exchanges between libraries where no other agreement applies.

Reprinted with permission from the American Library Association.

[Haworth co-indexing entry note]: "Appendix B. Supplementary Material to the National Interlibrary Loan Code." Hilyer, Lee Andrew. Co-published simultaneously in *Journal of Interlibrary Loan, Document Delivery & Electronic Reserve* (The Haworth Information Press, an imprint of The Haworth Press, Inc.) Vol. 16, No. 1/2, 2006, pp. 111-121; and: *Interlibrary Loan and Document Delivery: Best Practices for Operating and Managing Interlibrary Loan Services in All Libraries* (Lee Andrew Hilyer) The Haworth Information Press, an imprint of The Haworth Press, Inc., 2006, pp. 111-121. Single or multiple copies of this article are available for a fee from The Haworth Document Delivery Service [1-800-HAWORTH, 9:00 a.m. - 5:00 p.m. (EST). E-mail address: docdelivery@haworthpress.com].

http://www.haworthpress.com/web/JILDD
© 2006 by The Haworth Press, Inc. All rights reserved.
doi:10.1300/J474v16n01_10

This interlibrary loan code describes the responsibilities of libraries to each other when requesting material for users. Increasingly libraries are allowing users to request material directly from suppliers. This code makes provision for direct patron requesting and at the same time affirms the responsibility of the patron's library for the safety and return of the borrowed material, or for paying the cost of a non-returnable item sent directly to the patron.

1. Definition

This code is intended to cover transactions between two libraries. Transactions between libraries and commercial document suppliers or library fee-based services are contractual arrangements beyond the scope of these guidelines.

The terms "requesting library" and "supplying library" are used in preference to "borrowing" and "lending" to cover the exchange of copies as well as loans.

2. Purpose

Interlibrary loan is intended to complement local collections and is not a substitute for good library collections intended to meet the routine needs of users. Interlibrary loan is based on a tradition of sharing resources between various types and sizes of library and rests on the belief that no library, no matter how large or well supported, is self-sufficient in today's world. It is also evident that some libraries are net lenders and others are net borrowers, but the system of interlibrary loan still rests on the belief that all libraries should be willing to lend if they are willing to borrow.

3. Scope

The conduct of international interlibrary loan is regulated by the rules set forth in the IFLA document *International Lending: Principles and Guidelines for Procedure.*[2]

Although the U.S. shares a common border with Canada and Mexico, it is important to remember that these countries have their own library infrastructures and interlibrary loan codes. The *IFLA Principles and Guidelines* regulate the exchange of material between institutions across these borders. Further, U.S. librarians would be wise to inform themselves of customs requirements that take precedence over library agreements when material is shipped across these national borders as described in the Association of Research Libraries' *Transborder Interlibrary Loan: Shipping Interlibrary Loan Materials from the U.S. to Canada.*[3]

4. Responsibilities of the Requesting Library

4.1 Written Policies

A library's interlibrary loan borrowing policy should be available in a written format that is readily accessible to all library users. Whenever possible the borrowing policy should be posted on the library's Web site as well as is available in paper copy at public service desks or wherever other library user handouts are provided.

4.2 Confidentiality

Interlibrary loan transactions, like circulation transactions, are confidential library records. Interlibrary loan personnel are encouraged to be aware of local/state confidentiality rules and laws as they relate to interlibrary loan transactions. Appropriate steps, such as using identification numbers or codes rather than users' names, should be taken to maintain confidentiality. However, it is not a violation of this code to include a user's name on a request submitted to a supplier. Policies and procedures should be developed regarding the retention of interlibrary loan records and access to this information. Interlibrary loan personnel should also be aware of privacy issues when posting requests for assistance or using the text of interlibrary loan requests as procedural examples. ALA's Office for Intellectual Freedom has developed a number of policies regarding confidentiality of library records.[4]

ILL staff should adhere to the American Library Association's (ALA) Code of Ethics,[5] specifically principle III, that states: "We protect each library user's right to privacy and confidentiality with respect to information sought or received and resources consulted, borrowed, acquired or transmitted."

4.3 Responsibility for Unmediated Interlibrary Loan Requests

A requesting library that chooses to allow its users to order materials through interlibrary loan without mediation accepts responsibility for these requests as if they have been placed by library staff. The supplying library may assume that the user has been authenticated and authorized to place requests and that the requesting library assumes full responsibility for transaction charges, the safety and return of material, and the expense of replacement or repair.

4.4 Complete Bibliographic Citation

A good bibliographic description is the best assurance that the user will receive the item requested. Rather than detail these descriptive elements, the code requires the requesting library to include whatever data provides the best indication of the desired material, whether a string of numbers or an extensive bibliographic citation. The important point is that this description be exact enough to avoid unnecessary work on the part of the supplier and frustration on the part of the unrequited user. For example, journal title verification rather than article level verification would be sufficient.

4.5 Identifying Appropriate Suppliers

Requesting libraries should use all resources at their disposal to determine ownership of a particular title before sending a request to a potential supplier. Many libraries contribute their holdings to major bibliographic utilities such as DOCLINE, OCLC, and RLIN and make their individual catalogs freely available via the Internet. The interlibrary loan listserv (ILL-L@listserv.acns.nwu.edu) or other ILL-related lists are also excellent sources for the requesting library to verify and/or locate particularly difficult items.

The requesting library is encouraged to use resources such as the OCLC online Name Address Directory, Research Libraries Group's *Shares Participants and Interlibrary Loan Directory*,[6] and/or Leslie Morris' *Interlibrary Loan Policies Directory*[7] to determine lending policies before requesting material.

The requesting library should clearly state on the request an amount that meets or exceeds the charges of suppliers to which the request is sent. Libraries are encouraged to use electronic invoicing capabilities such as OCLC's Interlibrary Loan Fee Management (IFM) system or the Electronic Fund Transfer System used by medical libraries.

4.6 Sending Unverified Requests

Despite the requirements in Sec. 4.4 and 4.5 that an item should be completely and accurately described and located, the code recognizes that it is not always possible to verify and/or locate a particular item. For example, a request may be sent to a potential supplier with strong holdings in a subject or to the institution at which the working paper was written.

4.7 Transmitting the Request

The code recommends electronic communication. For many libraries, sending requests electronically means using the interlibrary loan messaging systems associated with DOCLINE, OCLC, RLIN, other products that use the ISO interlibrary loan Protocol, or structured e-mail requests.

Lacking the ability to transmit in this fashion, the requesting library should mail a completed ALA interlibrary loan request form, fax a request using ALA's *Guidelines and Procedures for Telefacsimile and Electronic Delivery of Interlibrary Loan Requests,*[8] or otherwise provide the same information via conventional letter or e-mail message.

Any special needs, such as for a particular edition, language, and/or rapid delivery, should be included on the request. The requesting library should include a street address, a postal box number, an Ariel address, a fax number, and/or an e-mail address to give the supplying library delivery options.

4.8 Copy Requests

The requesting library is responsible for complying with the provisions of Section 108(g)(2) Copyright Law[9] and the *Guidelines for the Proviso of Subsection 108(g)(2)* prepared by the National Commission on New Technological Uses of Copyrighted Works (the CONTU Guidelines).[10]

4.9 Responsibility of the Requester

The requesting library assumes a small but inherent risk when material is supplied through interlibrary loan. Although the percentage is very small, some material is lost or damaged at some point along the route from the supplier and back again. The requesting library's responsibility for this loss is based on the concept that if the request had not been made, the material would not have left the supplier's shelf, and thus would not have been put at risk. This section clearly delineates that the requesting library is responsible for the material from the time it leaves the supplying library until its safe return to the supplying library.

If the requesting library asks for delivery at a location away from the library (such as to the user's home), the requesting library is likewise responsible for the material during this delivery and return process. In any case, a final decision regarding replacement, repair, or compensation rests with the supplying library.

Although the code stipulates that the requesting library is required to pay if billed for a lost or damaged item, the supplying library is not necessarily required to charge for a lost item. In the case of lost material, the requesting and supplying libraries may need to work together to resolve the matter. For instance, the library shipping the material may need to initiate a trace with the delivery firm.

4.10 Due Date and Use Restrictions

This code makes a departure from earlier codes that described due dates in terms of a "loan period" which was interpreted as the length of time a requesting library could retain the material before returning it. The primary object of this section is to provide a clear definition of due date as the date the material must be checked in at the supplying library. This definition brings interlibrary loan practice into alignment with automated circulation procedures and is intended to facilitate interoperability of interlibrary loan and circulation applications.

The requesting library should develop a method for monitoring due dates so that material can be returned to and checked in at the supplying library by the due date assigned by the supplying library.

The requesting library is responsible for ensuring compliance with any use restrictions specified by the supplying library such as "library use only" or "no photocopying."

4.11 Renewals

When the supplying library denies a renewal request the material should be returned by the original due date.

4.12 Recalls

The response to a recall may be the immediate return of the material, or timely communication with the supplying library to negotiate a new due date.

When the material has been recalled, the requesting library is encouraged to return the material via an expedited delivery carrier such as UPS, FedEx, or USPS Priority Mail.

4.13 Shipping

Libraries shipping materials for interlibrary loan purposes should follow ALA's *Interlibrary Loan Packaging and Wrapping Guidelines*[11] and *ALA's Guidelines for Packaging and Shipping Microforms*.[12] If the supplying library states any special shipping or handling instructions, such as returning via a certain shipper, by priority mail, etc., the requesting library needs to comply with these instructions.

4.14 Suspension of Service

Repeated or egregious breaches of this code may result in the requesting library's inability to obtain material. Examples of actions that may result in suspension include lost or damaged books, allowing "library use only" books to leave the library, or failing to pay the supplier's charges.

5. Responsibilities of the Supplying Library

5.1 Lending Policy

The lending policy should be clear, detailed, and readily available to requesting libraries. The policy should include among other things, schedule of fees and charges, overdue fines, non-circulating items/categories, shipping instructions, calendar for service suspensions, penalties for late payments, etc.

The supplying library is encouraged to make its lending policy available in print, on the library's Web page, and, as appropriate, in the OCLC online Name Address Directory (NAD), RLG's *Shares Participants and Interlibrary Loan Directory*,[13] and Leslie Morris' *Interlibrary Loan Policies Directory*.[14]

The supplying library should be willing to fill requests for all types and classes of users, and all types of libraries, regardless of their size or geographic location.

5.2 Material Format

Supplying libraries are encouraged to lend as liberally as possible regardless of the format of the material requested. It is the obligation of the supplying library to consider the loan of material on a case-by-case basis. Supplying libraries are encouraged to lend audiovisual material, newspapers, and other categories of material that have traditionally been non-circulating.

Supplying libraries are encouraged to follow ACRL's *Guidelines for the Loan of Rare and Unique Materials*[15] and the *Guidelines for Interlibrary Loan of Audiovisual Formats*.[16]

If permitted by copyright law, the supplying library should consider providing a copy in lieu of a loan rather than giving a negative response.

Supplying libraries should be alert to license agreements for electronic resources that prohibit use of an electronic resource to fill copy requests.

5.3 Confidentiality

The supplying library has a responsibility to safeguard the confidentiality of the individual requesting the material. The sharing of the user's name between requesting and supplying library is not, of itself, a violation of confidentiality. However, the supplying library should not require the user's name if the requesting library chooses not to provide it. If the name is provided, the supplying library needs to take care not to divulge the identity of the person requesting the material.

5.4 Timely Processing

The supplying library has a responsibility to act promptly on all requests. If a supplying library cannot fill a request within a reasonable time then it should respond promptly. Some interlibrary loan messaging systems such as OCLC and DOCLINE have built-in time periods after which requests will either expire or be sent to another institution. The supplying library should respond before this time expires rather than allow requests to time-out.

Timely processing of a loan or copy may involve other library departments, such as circulation, copy services, and the mailroom. The interlibrary loan office is responsible for ensuring that material is delivered expeditiously, irrespective of internal library organizational responsibilities.

The supplying library should, when charging for materials, make every effort to allow for a variety of payment options. Payment through electronic crediting and debiting services such as OCLC's Interlibrary loan Fee Management (IFM) system or other non-invoicing payment forms such as IFLA vouchers should be encouraged. The supplying library that charges should make every effort to accept the use of vouchers, coupons, or credit cards. Paper invoices should be avoided if at all possible.

5.5 Identifying the Request

The supplying library should send enough identifying information with the material to allow the requesting library to identify the material and process the request quickly. Such information may include a copy of the request, the requestor's transaction number, or the user's ID or name. Failure to include identifying information with the material can unduly delay its processing and may risk the safety of the material.

Supplying libraries are encouraged to enclose an accurate and complete return-mailing label.

5.6 Use Restrictions and Due Date

Although it is the responsibility of the requesting library to ensure the safe treatment and return of borrowed material, the supplying library should provide specific instructions when it is lending material that needs special handling. These instructions might include the requirement that material be used only in a monitored special collections area, no photocopying, library use only, specific return packaging/shipping instructions, etc. The supplying library should not send "library use only" material directly to a user.

The supplying library should clearly indicate the date on which it expects the loan to be discharged in its circulation system. As explained in section 4.10 above, this code has moved away from the concept of a loan period, to a definite date that accommodates the sending and return of material as well as sufficient time for the use of the material. For example, under the previous code a supplying library may have given "four weeks use" as the "due date" with the expectation that the user would have that period of time to use the material. Under this code, a supplying library might establish a due date of six (6) weeks for the purpose of providing one (1) week for shipping, four (4) weeks for use, and one (1) week for the return trip and check-in.

5.7 Delivery and Packaging

The location specified by the requesting library may include the requesting library, a branch or departmental library, or the individual user.

The supplying library needs to take care that the material it sends out is properly packaged to protect the item from damage even though the requesting library will be held responsible for material damaged in shipment. The supplying library should also include any instructions on how it expects the material to be packaged on its return shipment. Supplying libraries should not give a postal box number as the return address if they are asking for return via UPS, FedEx, etc. Many supplying libraries find it safer and more cost effective to ship all material via expedited carriers.

The shipping library should follow ALA's *Interlibrary Loan Packaging and Wrapping Guidelines*[17] and ALA's *Guidelines for Packaging and Shipping Microforms.*[18]

Both the requesting and supplying libraries should work together when tracing a lost or damaged item if the commercial delivery firm is responsible for reimbursement for losses in transit.

5.8 Renewals

The supplying library should respond affirmatively or negatively to all renewal requests. The supplying library is encouraged to grant the renewal request if the material is not needed by a local user.

5.9 Recall

The supplying library may recall material at its discretion at any time. Increasingly, some libraries are finding it more effective to request the material on interlibrary loan for a local user rather than recall material in use by another library.

5.10 Service Suspension

A supplying library should not suspend service without first attempting to address the problem with the requesting library.

REFERENCES

1. Boucher, Virginia. *Interlibrary Loan Practices Handbook*. Chicago, IL: American Library Association, 1997. Though written in light of an earlier code, the *Practices Handbook* contains many useful and practical details on interlibrary loan procedures.

2. International Federation of Library Associations and Institutions. *International Lending: Principles and Guidelines for Procedure*. 1987. <http://www.ifla.org/VII/s15/pubs/pguide.htm>.

3. *Transborder Interlibrary Loan: Shipping Interlibrary Loan Materials from the U.S. to Canada*. 1995. <ftp://www.arl.org/ill.trans>.

4. American Library Association. Office for Intellectual Freedom. *Policy on Confidentiality of Library Records*. 1986. <http://www.ala.org/alaorg/oif/pol_conf.html>. American Library Association. Office for Intellectual Freedom. *Policy Concerning Confidentiality of Personally Identifiable Information about Library Users*. 1991. <http://www.ala.org/alaorg/oif/pol_user.html>.

5. American Library Association. Committee on Professional Ethics. *Code of Ethics*. Chicago, American Library Association, 1995. <http://www.ala.org/alaorg/oif/ethics.html>.

6. Research Libraries Group. *Shares Participants and Interlibrary Loan Directory*. 5th ed. 1996. <http://www.rlg.org/shares/illd.html>.

7. Morris, Leslie. *Interlibrary Loan Policies Directory*. 7th ed. New York: Neal-Schuman, 2001.

8. American Library Association. Reference and Adult Services Division. *Guidelines and Procedures for Telefacsimile and Electronic Delivery of Interlibrary Loan Requests*. 1993. <http://www.ala.org/rusa/stnd_telefax.html>.

9. Copyright Law of the United States of America Title 17 of the U.S. Code. <http://www.loc.gov/copyright/title17>.

10. National Commission on New Technological Uses of Copyrighted Works. *Guidelines for the Provision of Subsection 108(g) (2)*. <http://www.cni.org/docs/infopols/CONTU.html>.

11. American Library Association. Reference and User Services Association. *Interlibrary Loan Packaging and Wrapping Guidelines*. 1997. <http://www.ala.org/rusa/stnd_illpack.html>.

12. American Library Association. Association for Library Collections and Technical Services. *Guidelines for Packaging and Shipping Microforms*. 1989. <http://www.ala.org/alcts/publications/guidelines/packaging.html>.

13. RLG, op. cit.

14. Morris, op. cit.

15. American Library Association. Association of College and Research Libraries. Ad Hoc Committee on the Interlibrary Loan of Rate and Unique Materials. *Guidelines for the Loan of Rate and Unique Materials*. 1993. <http://www.ala.org/acrl/guides/loanrare.html>.

16. American Library Association. *Guidelines for Interlibrary Loan of Audiovisual Formats*. 1998. <http://www.ala.org/vrt/illguide.html>.

17. *Wrapping and Packaging Guidelines*, op. cit.

18. *Guidelines for Packaging and Shipping Microforms*, op. cit.

Appendix C

Statewide ILL Codes–Texas

TexShare (Texas) Interlibrary Loan Protocol
(http://www.texshare.edu)

1.0. Introduction

TexShare is a vision of shared intellectual resources, both physical and electronic, among academic and public libraries in Texas; the broader the participation in this endeavor, the greater the benefit to the entire group. This protocol encourages TexShare Libraries to be as generous as possible with each other while maintaining institutional priorities for interlibrary loan service. The goals of resource sharing and cooperation established by TexShare can best be achieved by removing as many barriers as possible from interlibrary loan service.

2.0. General Agreements

2.1 All participants agree to abide by the **National Interlibrary Loan Code**.

2.2 TexShare Libraries will adhere to the **Copyright Law of the United States (Title 17, U.S. Code)**, and the **CONTU** (National Commission on New Technological Uses of the Copyrighted Works;

The TexShare Interlibrary Loan Protocol was authored by the TexShare Interlibrary Loan Working Group. Reprinted with permission.

[Haworth co-indexing entry note]: "Appendix C. Statewide ILL Codes–Texas." Hilyer, Lee Andrew. Co-published simultaneously in *Journal of Interlibrary Loan, Document Delivery & Electronic Reserve* (The Haworth Information Press, an imprint of The Haworth Press, Inc.) Vol. 16, No. 1/2, 2006, pp. 123-132; and: *Interlibrary Loan and Document Delivery: Best Practices for Operating and Managing Interlibrary Loan Services in All Libraries* (Lee Andrew Hilyer) The Haworth Information Press, an imprint of The Haworth Press, Inc., 2006, pp. 123-132. Single or multiple copies of this article are available for a fee from The Haworth Document Delivery Service [1-800-HAWORTH, 9:00 a.m. - 5:00 p.m. (EST). E-mail address: docdelivery@haworthpress.com].

http://www.haworthpress.com/web/JILDD
doi:10.1300/J474v16n01_11

LC3.2L61/988;) Guidelines. Libraries obtaining a significant number of copies should consider registering with the **Copyright Clearance Center (CCC).**

2.3 TexShare libraries will enter lending policies in OCLC's Name Address Directory (NAD) and keep the record current.

2.4 TexShare Libraries are encouraged to lend materials in all formats. As a general guideline, TexShare Libraries will lend materials in any format that an on site patron could check out according to standard circulation policy unless the item is in high demand at the owning institution. Formats may include, but are not limited to:

Audiovisual materials (sound recording, video, slides)
Books (regardless of imprint date)
Computer software and data (diskettes, CD-ROMs)
Dissertations and theses (not to include archival copies)
Electronic journals (as licenses permit)
Genealogy (copies may be provided as an alternative to loan)
Government documents (local, state, US, foreign, and international)
Microforms (fiche, film, and card)
Photocopies (of any length)

2.5 TexShare Libraries will make every effort to ensure that no single library is unduly burdened and that interlibrary loan traffic is distributed equitably among the member libraries. To that end, each library will adhere to the attached **load leveling guidelines.**

2.6 TexShare will make available copies of the statistical reports on interlibrary loan activity through the **Chair of the Working Group** or the **Resource Sharing Consultant** at the Texas State Library and Archives Commission. Statistics will be posted periodically on the TexShare web site. These data will provide information on borrowing and lending patterns and serve as a guide for load leveling for each library. Interlibrary loan managers are encouraged to send requests to net borrowers and to avoid net lenders whenever possible. The cost of these statistical reports will be funded from the TexShare budget.

3.0. Access to Holdings

3.1 TexShare Libraries are encouraged to list and update their holdings in OCLC. All TexShare members that are full OCLC members must join the Texas Group (GAC) so that selective users will have access to their holdings. Libraries not currently full OCLC users or members of the GAC must participate in the GAC in order to send TexShare interlibrary loan requests. This will enable all TexShare Libraries to participate more fully in resource sharing.

3.2 Union List:

3.2.1 TexShare Libraries are encouraged to make their issue-specific serial holdings available on OCLC. If local data records for all serial titles cannot be included on the Union List, libraries should consider entering data for selected records.

3.2.2 Libraries that participate in union lists should update local data records for holdings on OCLC at least annually.

4.0. Delivery

4.1 Libraries are encouraged to use TExpress and Ariel as preferred delivery methods.

4.2 Ariel

4.2.1 Since many libraries provide electronic document delivery to their patrons, suppliers are strongly encouraged to use Ariel for delivery to facilitate this.

4.2.2 TexShare Libraries will keep Ariel equipment on all the time, so that Ariel transmissions can be received at any time.

4.2.3 Libraries using Ariel for delivery agree to the following terms:

4.2.3.1 Borrower will:

4.2.3.1.1 Check and request re-sends within one (1) working day of receipt or consider it a second request.

4.2.3.1.2 Use the header page supplied by the lender to re-quest re-sends and indicate why the re-send is required.

4.2.3.1.3 Request re-send with dither on if required to obtain good quality illustrations.

4.2.3.2 Lender will:

4.2.3.2.1 Re-transmit error pages within one working day.

4.2.3.2.2 Include header page with all transmissions includ-ing re-sends. Information to be included on header page:

4.2.3.2.2.1 Institution name and/or OCLC symbol or DocLINE identification

4.2.3.2.2.2 Patron name

4.2.3.2.2.3 OCLC, DocLINE, or other relevant interli-brary loan request numbers

4.2.3.2.2.4 Notification in the notes field when re-trans-mission is a re-send.

4.2.3.2.3 A separate header page should be used for each document. Send only one interlibrary loan request/document in each transmission.

4.2.3.2.4 Use dither on for transmitting or re-transmitting pages, with important illustrations at the request of the bor-rower.

4.2.3.2.5 If a document fails to transmit within 24 hours, the supplier may notify the requester and request a reboot of the system. The document can be sent by TExpress, mailed, faxed, or retained for Ariel transmission at the supplier's dis-cretion.

4.3 TExpress

4.3.1 TexShare libraries are encouraged to use TExpress for loans (and article copies when Ariel or fax is unavailable) because deliveries are fast, and TExpress reduces postage costs for all lenders. Refer to the **TExpress Shipping Guidelines** for details.

4.3.2 Padded envelopes or equivalent protection must be used for loans to ensure safe delivery. Refer to the **ALA Packaging Guidelines**.

4.3.3 The city hub number and the library site must both appear on the TExpress mailing label.

4.3.4 Participating TExpress libraries must prominently display their TExpress information in the following areas:

–The library's OCLC Name-Address Directory (NAD) record
–The library's OCLC constant data records as the first line of the: SHIP TO: field.

> : SHIP TO:
> 140-HOU VIA TEXPRESS/
> ILL/
> Rice University Library/
> 6100 Main St./
> Houston, TX 77005

4.3.5 If the requesting library wants to designate a branch library as the receiver of the loan, include the local symbol for the branch in the: SHIP TO: field.

> : SHIP TO:
> 129-HOU VIA TEXPRESS-Attn: FC/
> ILL/
> Fort Bend County Libraries/
> 1001 Golfbend Drive/
> Richmond, TX 77469

Lending libraries will include the symbol or name of the branch library in the Attention field on the TExpress label.

4.3.6 If libraries use TExpress to return non-ILL items, they must be clearly labeled inside the mailing envelope to indicate where the item should be routed at the receiving site, e.g., Circulation Department.

5.0. Processing Requests All requests must be processed through OCLC or DocLINE. Libraries which do not use OCLC currently must join Amigos as a general member and the Texas Group (GAC) which will allow OCLC access for interlibrary loan without requiring the use of OCLC for cataloging.

5.1 TexShare Libraries agree to:

5.1.1 Use the term COND to inform the borrower of citation errors. Use Reasons for No on all unfilled requests to indicate why the request was not filled.

5.1.2 Include the following information on TexShare requests:

5.1.2.1 The term "TexShare" in the affiliations field

5.1.2.2 Ariel address under e-mail or fax field

5.1.2.3 Fax number

5.1.2.4 Phone number

5.1.2.5 TExpress hub and site number as the first line in the :SHIP TO: address. See 4.3.4 for correct format. The TExpress address alone is not sufficient; the U.S. mail address must also be included.

5.1.2.6 The Lender will supply the interlibrary loan number and patron name with the loaned item.

5.2 Recommended borrowing strategies and the order in which to employ them are outlined in the attached **Guidelines for Load Leveling in TexShare.**

5.2.1 Libraries should use the **Custom Holdings** feature of OCLC to facilitate load leveling (See **Guidelines for Load Leveling in TexShare**).

5.2.2 Interlibrary loan staff will check for issue specific periodical holdings (using such resources as UTXL or other union lists) when available before placing requests. Adoption of this practice will reduce turnaround time for the borrowing library. It will limit the number of requests for materials not owned which are handled by the lending library. First Search Direct Requests for periodicals should be profiled for review by interlibrary loan staff for Union List verification.

5.2.3 Libraries that do not participate in the union list for serials should consider adding local data records for frequently requested serial titles.

5.3 Requests will be in one of the following two status groups. Processing is complete when the supplier has informed the requester that material has been shipped or cannot be supplied.

5.3.1 RUSH Requests:

5.3.1.1 Borrower will:

5.3.1.1.1 Indicate RUSH on the request.

5.3.1.1.2 Include the need by date and time.

5.3.1.1.3 Send the request via OCLC/DocLINE. Using OCLC/DocLINE will provide statistical data.

5.3.1.1.4 Fax, or transmit via Ariel, a copy of the OCLC/DocLINE request to the lender and follow up with a phone call, if necessary.

5.3.1.1.5 Indicate preferred method of delivery.

5.3.1.1.6 Agree to pay for overnight delivery, if this delivery method is required.

5.3.1.2 Lender will:

5.3.1.2.1 Process by need by date and time.

5.3.1.2.2 Use reasons for "no."

5.3.1.2.3 Send the item by a rush delivery method: FAX, Ariel, or TExpress (at the discretion of the borrower) for photocopies; TExpress, first class mail; or equivalent for other materials (at the discretion of the borrower); or overnight delivery if paid for by the borrower.

5.3.1.2.4 Reserve the right to refuse a RUSH request, if staffing or other factors prevent successful compliance.

5.3.2 REGULAR Requests (default): Routine handling; processing within three (3) working days; routine delivery method.

5.3.2.1 Borrower will:

Send request via OCLC/DocLINE.

5.3.2.2 Lender will:

Send the item by any of the following methods: TExpress, Ariel, FAX, or first class mail for photocopies; TExpress, UPS, or library rate mail for other materials.

5.4 The term RUSH will not be used routinely and will not be in the constant data record. If a lending library thinks a borrower is abusing RUSH, the lender will so notify the requester and/or ignore the RUSH status.

5.4.1 Libraries that refuse to supply RUSH processing cannot expect RUSH processing for their borrowing requests.

6.0. Lending Policies and Loan Periods The lending policies of TexShare Libraries with regard to one another will be as liberal as possible for the convenience of the borrowing clientele, and all such policies and restrictions will be honored by the borrowing library under all circumstances.

6.1 TexShare Libraries agree to the following minimum guidelines. Libraries wishing to follow more liberal policies may do so.

6.1.1 The normal loan period for materials borrowed from another TexShare Library is a minimum of four weeks, including time required for delivery and return. Longer loan periods and renewals will be permitted at the discretion of the lending library. Lending libraries may require a shorter loan period for specific materials.

6.1.2 Recalls of materials on interlibrary loan will be honored as promptly as it is possible to retrieve materials from clientele.

7.0. Communication At least one staff member from each TexShare Library's interlibrary loan unit will join and participate in the **LoanStar discussion group** on the Internet. This group will serve as a think tank, information dissemination mechanism, and survey instrument for the interlibrary loan services of TexShare Libraries.

8.0. Costs

8.1 The goal is for TexShare Libraries not to charge for interlibrary loan services and for all libraries to participate. TexShare Libraries will not charge each other overdue fines or processing fees for lost materials.

8.2 Borrowing libraries will be responsible for the replacement costs of items lost or damaged (replacement or repair cost of the item only; not additional processing fees). Borrowing libraries are responsible for items from the time they are shipped by the lending library until the lending library receives them upon return in accordance with the **National Interlibrary Loan Code**.

8.3 Lending libraries will not charge more than the price that appears in Books in Print for lost books that are still in print. Out-of-print materials may be subject to the Lending library's default cost for lost books. Lending libraries are encouraged to permit borrowing libraries to replace lost or damaged books in kind (same title, same publication date, same format as lost item). In no case may the default replacement cost be higher than what the lending library would charge its own patrons for a lost book.

8.4 When requests have been placed by one library on behalf of another (referrals), the library receiving the material is responsible for all costs in case of loss or damage. However, if the receiving library is not responsive to requests for return, replacement or payment for lost or damaged borrowed materials, the incident should be brought to the attention of the referring library.

8.5 Lending libraries should notify borrowing libraries promptly when materials are overdue. Invoices for lost materials should normally follow within three months. Invoices for lost books should be paid promptly unless other arrangements are made with the lending library.

8.6 Filling interlibrary loan requests sent by fee-based entities operated by TexShare Libraries is not covered by this Protocol. Such entities will be charged for interlibrary loan services. TexShare Libraries operating fee-based document delivery services will clearly identify requests for paying clients on interlibrary loan request forms.

9.0. Review and Assessment

9.1 The Working Group will periodically review and revise the protocol. The Working Group will act as an advisory group on protocol issues to TexShare management.

(Revised January 22, 2003)

On the web at:
http://www.texshare.edu/programs/ill/illprotocol.html.

Appendix D

Reciprocal Agreement

Smithfield Library
OCLC : **TXH** DOCLINE: **TXUUTO**

Reciprocal Interlibrary Loan Agreement

_____ and the Smithfield Library agree to cooperate in a reciprocal agreement with the following provisions:

1. Book loans at no charge.
2. Photocopies at no charge.
3. Special consideration for Rush requests.

Revisions to this agreement may be made in writing with the consent of both libraries. Either library may terminate this agreement at any time by providing one week's written notice to the other.

Please complete the information below and return a copy of this form to the PC/ILL Department by ARIEL, fax, or mail.

[Haworth co-indexing entry note]: "Appendix D. Reciprocal Agreement." Hilyer, Lee Andrew. Co-published simultaneously in *Journal of Interlibrary Loan, Document Delivery & Electronic Reserve* (The Haworth Information Press, an imprint of The Haworth Press, Inc.) Vol. 16, No. 1/2, 2006, pp. 133-134; and: *Interlibrary Loan and Document Delivery: Best Practices for Operating and Managing Interlibrary Loan Services in All Libraries* (Lee Andrew Hilyer) The Haworth Information Press, an imprint of The Haworth Press, Inc., 2006, pp. 133-134. Single or multiple copies of this article are available for a fee from The Haworth Document Delivery Service [1-800-HAWORTH, 9:00 a.m. - 5:00 p.m. (EST). E-mail address: docdelivery@haworthpress.com].

http://www.haworthpress.com/web/JILDD
© 2006 by The Haworth Press, Inc. All rights reserved.
doi:10.1300/J474v16n01_12

Interlibrary Loan Department
Smithfield Library, Rm 321
Smith University
458 Johnson St.
Smith, TX 70011
713-555-1212
713-555-4134 (Fax)
ill@smithu.edu
http://www.smithu.edu/Library/ILL
Hours: 8 a.m.-5 p.m. M-F

Appendix E

ILLiad E-Mail and Print Templates

The templates provided on the following pages are samples of some of the available templates in ILLiad, all of which are customizable to a department's particular specifications.

Customization allows ILL departments to "personalize" communications with their patrons and, in the case of print templates, allows a department to increase efficiency and effectiveness by organizing forms according to their own needs.

Templates can include almost any field from the ILLiad database and can also include extras such as URLs to policy documents, copyright resources, or other information.

E-mail templates are easily edited with a basic text editor such as Notepad, while the print templates should be edited from within Microsoft WORD®.

Templates reprinted with permission from the HAM-TMC Library.

[Haworth co-indexing entry note]: "Appendix E. ILLiad E-Mail and Print Templates." Hilyer, Lee Andrew. Co-published simultaneously in *Journal of Interlibrary Loan, Document Delivery & Electronic Reserve* (The Haworth Information Press, an imprint of The Haworth Press, Inc.) Vol. 16, No. 1/2, 2006, pp. 135-144; and: *Interlibrary Loan and Document Delivery: Best Practices for Operating and Managing Interlibrary Loan Services in All Libraries* (Lee Andrew Hilyer) The Haworth Information Press, an imprint of The Haworth Press, Inc., 2006, pp. 135-144. Single or multiple copies of this article are available for a fee from The Haworth Document Delivery Service [1-800-HAWORTH, 9:00 a.m. - 5:00 p.m. (EST). E-mail address: docdelivery@haworthpress.com].

http://www.haworthpress.com/web/JILDD
© 2006 by The Haworth Press, Inc. All rights reserved.
doi:10.1300/J474v16n01_13

E-MAIL TEMPLATES

New Patron Registration

YOU ARE NOW REGISTERED WITH HAM-TMC LIBRARY's <#SystemName>.

You may want to save this message for future reference.

Thank you for registering with the PC/ILL <#SystemName>.
You provided the following information:

Personal Information for <#Username>

Name: <#FirstName> <#Lastname>
Department: <#Department>

Your Mailing Address is:
<#Address> <#Address2>
<#City> <#State> <#Zip>

Your phone number is: <#Phone>

We will notify you by EMAIL when an item is received, or is ready for pickup from our website.

You can modify your personal information at any time by logging onto your account and changing your user information.

You can find us on the Web by going to:

<#SystemURL>

If you need assistance or did not authorize this registration and wish to have it canceled please send e-mail to:

<#BorrowingEMailAddress>

Cordially,

Photocopy/Interlibrary Loan Department
Houston Academy of Medicine–Texas Medical Center Library

Thank You for Using Our Services!

Delivery Notification (ILL and Photocopy Service)

Dear <#FirstName> <#LastName>

An article you requested:

TN: <#TransactionNumber> Your Reference: <#CitedTitle>
Journal: <#PhotoJournalTitle>. <#PhotoJournalYear>.
Article: <#PhotoArticleTitle>
Author: <#PhotoArticleAuthor>
Citation Details: <#PhotoJournalVolume> (<#PhotoJournalIssue>):
<#PhotoJournalInclusivePages>.
Requested Delivery Method: <#ShippingOptions>

is now ready for delivery.

–If you selected FAX or MAIL delivery, the item will be sent via your stated delivery method.

–If you selected PICKUP, the item is ready for pickup at the Circulation Desk.

–If you originally selected WEB, we're sorry, but electronic delivery is not available for this item. You can pick up the material you requested at the Circulation Desk, and we apologize for any inconvenience.

The cost for this material is: $<#BillingAmount>.

If you have questions or comments, please do not hesitate to contact us!

Cordially,

Photocopy/Interlibrary Loan Department
Houston Academy of Medicine–Texas Medical Center Library
<#GeneralEMailAddress>
Phone: <#GeneralPhone>

Thank You for Using Our Services!

Electronic Delivery Notification

Dear <#FirstName> <#LastName>,

An article you requested:

TN: <#TransactionNumber> (Your Reference: <#CitedTitle>)
Journal: <#PhotoJournalTitle>. <#PhotoJournalYear>.
Article: <#PhotoArticleTitle>
Author: <#PhotoArticleAuthor>
Citation Details: <#PhotoJournalVolume> (<#PhotoJournalIssue>):
<#PhotoJournalInclusivePages>.

has been posted to our secure website and is available for viewing.

You can retrieve this item by logging on to <#SystemURL> and choosing the RETRIEVE POSTED ARTICLES option from the main menu.

Electronic articles are available in PDF format and require the Adobe Acrobat Reader, which is available for download at http://www.adobe.com.

Please note that PDF files are available for 15 days from the date of this e-mail. Please review and print your document as soon as possible.

The cost for this material is: $<#BillingAmount>.

If you have any questions about electronic delivery, please do not hesitate to contact us.

Cordially,

Photocopy/Interlibrary Loan Department
Houston Academy of Medicine–Texas Medical Center Library
<#GeneralEmailAddress>
Phone: <#GeneralPhone>

Thank You for Using Our Services!

Custom Notification E-Mail (Need Cost Approval)

The HAM-TMC Library uses a two-tier pricing structure, and occasionally we cannot supply an item to a patron at their desired fee level. We use this e-mail to notify them that the material's cost will be higher than expected and to obtain their approval for requesting the item at the higher price.

AWAITING COST APPROVAL–Please respond!

Dear <#FirstName> <#LastName>

An item that you requested:

TN: <#TransactionNumber> Your Reference: <#CitedTitle>
Loan Title: <#LoanTitle>
Loan Author: <#LoanAuthor>
Article Title: <#PhotoArticleTitle>
Article Author: <#PhotoArticleAuthor>
Journal Title: <#PhotoJournalTitle>

is not available at the cost limit you selected–see below for more information:

[   ] The item is not available at the $4.00 Local Network interlibrary loan price. Do you want to raise your maximum cost to $14.00?

[   ] You selected a $4.00 interlibrary loan level. This item is owned by the HAM-TMC Library and can be copied for you at a cost of $8.00, or you can come into the library and make your own copies.

If you have any questions about this notice, please e-mail or call our office. If we do not hear from you within one week, we will cancel the request.

Cordially,

Photocopy/Interlibrary Loan Department
Houston Academy of Medicine–Texas Medical Center Library

Thank You for Using Our Services!

PRINT TEMPLATES

Article Slips for Borrowing

Houston Academy of Medicine–Texas Medical Center Library
Photocopy/Interlibrary Loan Department

Service: **INTERLIBRARY LOAN**   RMS TN: «TRANSACTIO»   Delivery: «SHIPPINGOP»
«SYSTEMID»: «ILLNUMBER»   **Level: «RUSH»**   Username: «USERNAME»

«FIRSTNAME» «LASTNAME» / Due: $____   Email: «EMAILADDRE»
«DESCRIPTIO»   Your Reference: «CITEDTITLE»
«ADDRESS»   Telephone: «PHONE»
«ADDRESS2»   Fax: «FAX»
«CITY» «STATE» «ZIP»   Library Card Number: «SSN»

Citation Information:

UI/PMID: «ESPNUMBER»
Journal/Book/AV Title: «PHOTOJOURN»
Volume: «PHOTOJOU_1» **Issue:** «PHOTOJOU_2» **Pages:** «PHOTOJOU_5» **Date:** «PHOTOJOU_4»
Article/Chapter Title: «PHOTOART_1»
Author(s)(of article/chapter): «PHOTOARTIC»

Copyright Information:

Warning Concerning Copyright Restrictions

The Copyright law of the United States (Title 17, United States Code) governs the making of photocopies or other reproductions of copyrighted materials. Under certain conditions specified in the law, libraries and archives are authorized to furnish a photocopy or other reproduction. One of the specified conditions is that the photocopy or reproduction is not to be "used for any purpose other than private study, scholarship, or research."

If a user makes a request for, or later uses, a photocopy or reproduction for purposes in excess of "fair use," that user may be liable for copyright infringement. *The HAM-TMC Library reserves the right to refuse to accept a request if, in its judgment, the fulfillment of the request would involve violation of the copyright law.*

For more information on copyright, consult the websites of the US Copyright Office (http://www.loc.gov/copyright) or the Copyright Clearance Center (http://www.copyright.com).

Billing Information:

Supplying Library: «LENDINGLIB»   **SOLOMON ID:** «NUMBER»

Amount Due This Transaction: (Patron Max Cost: «MAXCOST»)
$«BILLINGAMO»
Type: «TYPE»   **Number:** «ACCOUNTNO» / Ex. «CCEXPIRATI»

How to Contact Us:

Photocopy/Interlibrary Loan Department, HAM-TMC Library
Office Hours: «GENERALHOU»
Telephone: «BORROWINGP»
Fax: «GENERALFAX»
Email: «GENERALEMA»

Log on to the RMS anytime to check the status of your orders!
http://illiadw.library.tmc.edu/

Loan Slips for Borrowing

Houston Academy of Medicine–Texas Medical Center Library
Photocopy/Interlibrary Loan Department

Service: **INTERLIBRARY LOAN**   RMS TN: **«TRANSACTIO»**   Delivery: **«SHIPPINGOP»**
«SYSTEMID»: «ILLNUMBER»   Level: **«RUSH»**   Username: **«USERNAME»**

«FIRSTNAME» «LASTNAME» / Due: $____   Email: «EMAILADDRE»
«DESCRIPTIO»   Your Reference: «CITEDTITLE»
«ADDRESS»   Telephone: «PHONE»
«ADDRESS2»   Fax: «FAX»
«CITY» «STATE» «ZIP»   Library Card Number: «SSN»

Citation Information:

UI/PMID: «ESPNUMBER»
Book/AV Title: «LOANTITLE»
Author: «LOANAUTHOR»
Publisher: «LOANPUBLIS», «LOANPLACE», «LOANDATE»

DUE DATE: «DUEDATE» RENEWALS ALLOWED: «RENEWALSAL»

Billing Information:

Supplying Library: «LENDINGLIB»   **SOLOMON ID:** «NUMBER»

Amount Due This Transaction: (Patron Max Cost: «MAXCOST»)
$«BILLINGAMO»
Type: «TYPE»   **Number:** «ACCOUNTNO» / Ex.
«CCEXPIRATI»

How to Contact Us:

Photocopy/Interlibrary Loan Department, HAM-TMC Library
Office Hours: «GENERALHOU»
Telephone: «BORROWINGP»
Fax: «GENERALFAX»
Email: «GENERALEMA»

Log on to the RMS anytime to check the status of your orders!
http://illiadw.library.tmc.edu/

Pick Slips for Library Photocopy Service (Document Delivery)

Houston Academy of Medicine–Texas Medical Center Library Photocopy/Interlibrary Loan Department

Service: **PHOTOCOPY SERVICE**   RMS TN: «TRANSACTIO»   Delivery: «SHIPPINGOP»

«SYSTEMID»: «ILLNUMBER»   Level: «RUSH»   Username: «USERNAME»

«FIRSTNAME» «LASTNAME» / Due: Email: «EMAILADDRE»
$«BILLINGAMO» «TYPE»   Your Reference: «CITEDTITLE»
«ADDRESS»   Telephone: «PHONE»
«ADDRESS2»   Fax: «FAX»
«CITY» «STATE» «ZIP»   Library Card Number: «SSN»

Citation Information:

UI/PMID: «ESPNUMBER»
Journal/Book/AV Title: «PHOTOJOURN»
Volume: «PHOTOJOU_1» **Issue:** «PHOTOJOU_2» **Pages:** «PHOTOJOU_5» **Date:** «PHOTOJOU_4»
Article/Chapter Title: «PHOTOART_1»
Author(s)(of article/chapter): «PHOTOARTIC»

Copyright Information:

Warning Concerning Copyright Restrictions

The Copyright law of the United States (Title 17, United States Code) governs the making of photocopies or other reproductions of copyrighted materials. Under certain conditions specified in the law, libraries and archives are authorized to furnish a photocopy or other reproduction. One of the specified conditions is that the photocopy or reproduction is not to be "used for any purpose other than private study, scholarship, or research."

If a user makes a request for, or later uses, a photocopy or reproduction for purposes in excess of "fair use," that user may be liable for copyright infringement. *The HAM-TMC Library reserves the right to refuse to accept a request if, in its judgment, the fulfillment of the request would involve violation of the copyright law.*

For more information on copyright, consult the websites of the US Copyright Office (http://www.loc.gov/copyright) or the Copyright Clearance Center (http://www.copyright.com).

Billing Information:

Supplying Library: «LENDINGLIB»   **SOLOMON ID:** «NUMBER»

Total Amount Due: $«BILLINGAMO»   (Patron Max Cost: «MAXCOST»)

Type: «TYPE»   **Number:** «ACCOUNTNO»

How to Contact Us:

Photocopy/Interlibrary Loan Department, HAM-TMC Library
Office Hours: «GENERALHOU»
Telephone: «BORROWINGP»
Fax: «GENERALFAX»
Email: «GENERALEMA»

Log on to the RMS anytime to check the status of your orders!
http://illiadw.library.tmc.edu/

Article Slips for Lending

HAM-TMC LIBRARY INTERLIBRARY LENDING
ARTICLE/PHOTOCOPY

ILLiad TN: «TRANSACTIO»
ILL Number: «ILLNUMBER»

Shipping Address:
«LIBRARYNAM»
«ADDRESS1»
«ADDRESS2»
«ADDRESS3»
«ADDRESS4»

Borrower: «LENDERSTRI» **System:** «SYSTEMID»

Maxcost: «MAXCOST»

Lending String: «LENDINGSTR»

Patron: «PATRON»

Journal Title: «PHOTOJOURN»

Volume: «PHOTOJOU_1» **Issue:** «PHOTOJOU_2»
Month/Year: «PHOTOJOU_3»
«PHOTOJOU_4»**Pages:** «PHOTOJOU_5»

Article Author: «PHOTOARTIC»

Article Title: «PHOTOART_1»

NOTICE:
**THIS MATERIAL MAY BE PROTECTED BY
UNITED STATES COPYRIGHT LAW
(TITLE 17, U.S.C.)**

(S) Batch: (S) Invoice #:

Solomon-ID:
Billing Category: «BILLINGC_1»
EFTS: «EFTS»

Thursday, July 28, 2005

Call #/Location: «CALLNUMBER»

Reasons-for-Non-Supply

___ BDY (At Bindery)
___ CST (Cost exceeds stated maxcost)
___ INC (Not as Cited)
___ LAC (Lacking volume/issue)
___ LOS (Lost)
___ NYR (Not Yet Received)
___ NOS (Not on Shelf)
___ NOT (Title Not Owned)
___ OTH (Other)
Specify:_____
DELIVERY: «SHIPPINGOP»
«SPECINS»

Fax: «FAX»
Ariel: «ARIELADDRE»
Phone: «PHONE»

This document has been supplied to you from:

OCLC: **«OCLCSYMBOL»**
DOCLINE: **«DOCLINESYM»**

«INSTITUTIO»
«LIBRARYN_1»
«LENDINGADD»
«LENDINGA_1»
«LENDINGCIT», «LENDINGSTA»
«LENDINGZIP»

Hours: «LENDINGHOU»
Phone: «LENDINGPHO»
Fax: «LENDINGFAX»
ARIEL: «LENDINGARI»
Email: «LENDINGEMA»

Thank You for Using Our Services!

**THIS IS NOT AN INVOICE!
PLEASE WAIT TO BE BILLED.**

Loan Slips for Lending

HAM-TMC INTERLIBRARY LENDING LOAN

ILLiad TN: «TRANSACTIO»

«TRANSACTIO»

ILL Number: «ILLNUMBER»

«ILLNUMBER»

Shipping Address:
«LIBRARYNAM»
«ADDRESS1»
«ADDRESS2»
«ADDRESS3»
«ADDRESS4»

Borrower: «LENDERSTRI» System: «SYSTEMID»
Due Date: «DUEDATE»
Maxcost: «MAXCOST»

Lending String: «LENDINGSTR»

Patron: «PATRON»

Title: «LOANTITLE»

Author: «LOANAUTHOR»

Publication Info:
«LOANPUBLIS» «LOANDATE»

PLEASE RETURN THIS SLIP
WITH MATERIAL.

(S) Batch: (S) Invoice #:

Solomon-ID:
Billing Category: «BILLINGC_1»
EFTS: «EFTS»

Thursday, July 28, 2005

Call #/Location: «CALLNUMBER»

Reasons-for-Non-Supply

___ USE (In Use – N/A for Loan)
___ CST (Cost exceeds stated maxcost)
___ INC (Not as Cited)
___ LAC (Lacking)
___ LOS (Lost)
___ NCR (Non-Circulating)
___ NOS (Not On Shelf)
___ ORD (On Order – Not Yet Received)
___ NOT (Not Owned)
___ OTH (Other)
Specify:_____

DELIVERY: «SHIPPINGOP»
«SPECINS»

Fax: «FAX»
Ariel: «ARIELADDRE»
Phone: «PHONE»

PLEASE RETURN MATERIALS TO:

OCLC: **«OCLCSYMBOL»**
DOCLINE: **«DOCLINESYM»**

«INSTITUTIO»
«LIBRARYN_1»
«LENDINGADD»
«LENDINGA_1»
«LENDINGCIT», «LENDINGSTA»
«LENDINGZIP»

Hours: «LENDINGHOU»
Phone: «LENDINGPHO»
Fax: «LENDINGFAX»
ARIEL: «LENDINGARI»
Email: «LENDINGEMA»

Thank You for Using Our Services!

THIS IS <u>NOT</u> AN INVOICE!
PLEASE WAIT TO BE BILLED.

Appendix F

ILL Technology Directory

Below are the websites of selected vendors of computer software and hardware that might be of use in an ILL department. This is a selective list and by no means exhaustive. Check the websites listed below for more information on the products and services available.

One special note: Due to the rise of computer threats like viruses, worms, spyware and malware, ILL departments, in cooperation with their IT departments, must take the necessary precautions to protect computer workstations and networks.

SOFTWARE

Protection

Ad-Aware (http://www.lavasoftusa.com/software/adaware/)
A program you can use to remove ADWARE (unwanted advertisements and tracking) from your system.

SpyBot Search & Destroy
(http://www.safer-networking.org/en/download/index.html)
SpyBot removes malicious software programs commonly known as "spyware."

[Haworth co-indexing entry note]: "Appendix F. ILL Technology Directory." Hilyer, Lee Andrew. Co-published simultaneously in *Journal of Interlibrary Loan, Document Delivery & Electronic Reserve* (The Haworth Information Press, an imprint of The Haworth Press, Inc.) Vol. 16, No. 1/2, 2006, pp. 145-147; and: *Interlibrary Loan and Document Delivery: Best Practices for Operating and Managing Interlibrary Loan Services in All Libraries* (Lee Andrew Hilyer) The Haworth Information Press, an imprint of The Haworth Press, Inc., 2006, pp. 145-147. Single or multiple copies of this article are available for a fee from The Haworth Document Delivery Service [1-800-HAWORTH, 9:00 a.m. - 5:00 p.m. (EST). E-mail address: docdelivery@haworthpress.com].

http://www.haworthpress.com/web/JILDD
doi:10.1300/J474v16n01_14

Windows Update
(http://v4.windowsupdate.microsoft.com/en/default.asp)
By installing the latest updates to your Windows® operating system, you can ensure that your workstations have the most current security protection.

WEB

Internet Explorer 6 or higher
(http://www.microsoft.com/windows/ie/default.mspx)

Netscape Navigator 7.0 or higher
(http://www.netscape.com)

Mozilla or Firefox
(http://www.mozilla.org)

Opera
(http://www.opera.com/)

Lynx (text-based browser)
(http://lynx.browser.org/)

Plug-Ins

Java plug-in for browser
(http://java.sun.com/)

Flash plug-in for browser
(http://www.macromedia.com/software/flashplayer/)

Development Tools

Macromedia Dreamweaver
(http://www.macromedia.com/software/dreamweaver)

CoffeeCup HTML Editor
(http://www.coffeecup.com/html-editor/)

Helper Applications

Adobe Acrobat reader or Acrobat 6.0 (full version)
(http://www.adobe.com)

HARDWARE

Scanners

Fujitsu
(http://www.fcpa.com/products/scanners/)

Hewlett-Packard
(http://www.hp.com/united-states/consumer/gateway/fax_copiers_scanners.html)

Minolta
(http://konicaminolta.us/)
Konica-Minolta makes the popular "face-up" scanners (PS3000 and PS7000).

Index

BOOK ORDER FORM!

Order a copy of this book with this form or online at:
http://www.haworthpress.com/store/product.asp?sku= 5743

Interlibrary Loan and Document Delivery
Best Practices for Operating and Managing
Interlibrary Loan Services in All Libraries

_____ in softbound at $19.95 ISBN-13: 978-0-7890-3129-7 / ISBN-10: 0-7890-3129-9.
_____ in hardbound at $39.95 ISBN-13: 978-0-7890-3128-0 / ISBN-10: 0-7890-3128-0.

COST OF BOOKS _____

POSTAGE & HANDLING _____
US: $4.00 for first book & $1.50
for each additional book
Outside US: $5.00 for first book
& $2.00 for each additional book.

SUBTOTAL _____
In Canada: add 7% GST. _____

STATE TAX _____
CA, IL, IN, MN, NJ, NY, OH, PA & SD residents
please add appropriate local sales tax.

FINAL TOTAL _____
If paying in Canadian funds, convert
using the current exchange rate,
UNESCO coupons welcome.

❑**BILL ME LATER:**
Bill-me option is good on US/Canada/
Mexico orders only; not good to jobbers,
wholesalers, or subscription agencies.

❑**Signature** _____

Payment Enclosed: $ _____

❑ **PLEASE CHARGE TO MY CREDIT CARD:**
❑Visa ❑MasterCard ❑AmEx ❑Discover
❑Diner's Club ❑Eurocard ❑JCB

Account #_____

Exp Date _____

Signature _____
(Prices in US dollars and subject to change without notice.)

PLEASE PRINT ALL INFORMATION OR ATTACH YOUR BUSINESS CARD
Name
Address
City   State/Province   Zip/Postal Code
Country
Tel   Fax

May we use your e-mail address for confirmations and other types of information? ❑Yes ❑No We appreciate receiving
your e-mail address. Haworth would like to e-mail special discount offers to you, as a preferred customer.
We will never share, rent, or exchange your e-mail address. We regard such actions as an invasion of your privacy.

Order from your **local bookstore** or directly from
The Haworth Press, Inc. 10 Alice Street, Binghamton, New York 13904-1580 • USA
Call our toll-free number (1-800-429-6784) / Outside US/Canada: (607) 722-5857
Fax: 1-800-895-0582 / Outside US/Canada: (607) 771-0012
E-mail your order to us: orders@haworthpress.com

For orders outside US and Canada, you may wish to order through your local
sales representative, distributor, or bookseller.
For information, see http://haworthpress.com/distributors

(Discounts are available for individual orders in US and Canada only, not booksellers/distributors.)

Please photocopy this form for your personal use.
www.HaworthPress.com

BOF06